Missing in Manila

A Former Detective Investigates Claims that "It's More Fun in the Philippines!"

Natalie Vellacott

Copyright

Copyright Natalie Vellacott 2017

ISBN (Createspace): 9781546389361

This account is a true story. However, some names may have been changed to protect the identities of individuals. This book is not for profit with all author royalties being returned to Christian ministry.

All rights reserved. The whole of this work, including all text and illustrations, is protected by copyright. No part of it may be copied, altered, adapted or otherwise exploited in any way without express prior permission, unless in accordance with the provisions of the Copyright Designs and Patents Act 1988 or in order to photocopy or make duplicating masters of those pages so indicated, without alteration and including copyright notices, for the express purpose of instruction and examination. No parts of this work may otherwise be loaded, stored, manipulated, reproduced, or transmitted in any form or by any means, electronic or mechanical, including photocopying and recording, or by any information storage and retrieval system, without prior written permission from the publisher, on behalf of the copyright holder. The rights of Natalie Vellacott to be identified as the author and illustrator of this work have been asserted by them in accordance with the Copyright, Designs and Patents Act 1988.

Contents

Introduction 6

House Hunting in a Hurry 11

Finding a Table..15

Always be Prepared...21

Rudely Awakened 25

Too Much to Handle?...31

He Has a Wife Already! 38

How's the Weather? 41

The Kitten and the Cockroach..........................44

Language Learning..48

Bureaucratic Nonsense 52

The Fun Side 56

The Criminal Underworld 60

The City Awakens 63

Speed, Safety and Suspended Conductors.......67

Drop-In Dilemma 72

Monday Mayhem 76

Seventeen Jackets Please...................................81

The 29kg Girl 85

Death Comes to Cubao.......................................88

What's That Smell?...93

Camp Chaos 98

The Big House..103

Grandma Goes Rogue 109

Evicted! 113

Milestones 117

Ramiro: Too Young to Die 123

A Brief Respite 128

Tacloban Typhoon 132

Claustrophobic Cages 137

Pregnant and Homeless 140

The Bali Conspiracy 143

Luxurious Living 149

Hypothermic in Sagada 151

Decision Time 155

Reverse Culture Shock 159

About the Author 163

Natalie's Personal Story 165

The Wordless Book 168

Missionary in Manila 5

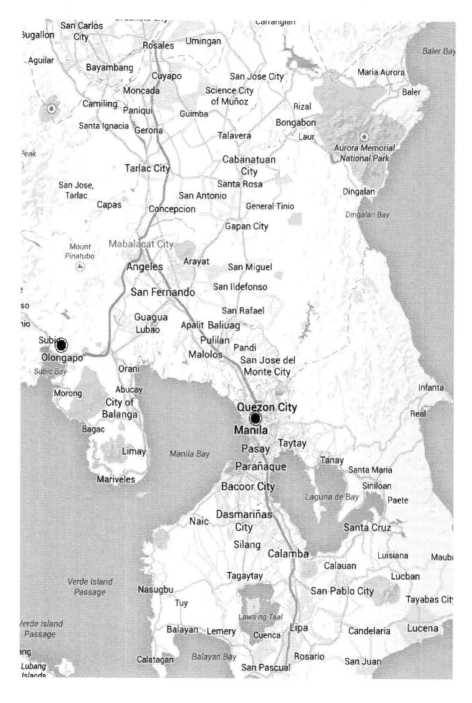

Introduction

I recently read *These Strange Ashes* by Elisabeth Elliot and realised afresh that many valuable lessons are learned in the first few years of missionary service. Prior to moving to live and work in the Philippines in December 2013, I had served for two years on-board Logos Hope—a Christian missionary ship. However, moving to the other side of the world alone and without an organisation was something entirely different. I was truly independent and about to be fully immersed in Filipino culture, whether I was ready for it or not.

My debut book *They're Rugby Boys, Don't You Know?* detailed my work in Olongapo City with Filipino street teenage boys that had begun whilst I was on Logos Hope. They were locally termed "rugby boys"—rugby was the name of the solvent they were abusing. I had returned independently to Olongapo after my commitment on the ship concluded with the intention of continuing to work with the boys. I was hoping to find a partner church to support the ministry to them. By this stage, some of the boys were in rehab in Manila so the plan was to prepare for their eventual release and to work with their families in the meantime.

Having failed to find a suitable church in Olongapo, at the end of my first book, I was in the process of relocating to the Philippine capital, Manila. I moved primarily to join Cubao Reformed Baptist Church which had been recommended to me by several friends in England. As it turned out, I hadn't been ready for the trials that had awaited me on my return to Olongapo—church politics and loose theology, being elevated as a foreign missionary there to save the world, difficulties obtaining a missionary VISA without an established organisation, and my eyes being opened to people and situations that were not as they had seemed when I had first met them.

I had been channelled initially into a Bible Baptist church on the remote outskirts of Olongapo City and rented an apartment nearby. From the city, access was only via an extremely long, steep, winding road that appeared to go on for miles. Taxis were reluctant to make the trip, preferring shorter, more lucrative journeys. I resorted at times to doing the unthinkable for a white foreigner—walking briskly up the side of the busy main road whilst attempting to thumb a lift as the locals gawped at me. Filipinos rarely walked anywhere. Once, I made the mistake of taking a tricycle with a sidecar to get home. It was a hair-raising experience as we bumped and jolted along. I thought the groaning and protesting engine was going to give up as we inched along at ridiculously low speeds. We were over-taken by much larger vehicles that threatened to push us over the edge of the gaping precipice and into a ravine. There was evidence of head-on collisions between buses on this dangerous stretch of road and people had been killed when vehicles had plummeted down the embankment.

The members of this first church saw me as some sort of miraculous answer to prayer—they had been praying for assistance with their outreach for a long time. I tried to downplay the fuss they were making. Unbeknownst to me, there had been a recent, acrimonious split in the church. Former members refused to speak to each other in the street, some even hid to avoid the confrontation. The pastor was determined to get his church family back together, whatever it took. But, the half that had left had been "poached" by Koreans who had established lively new churches in the area. The rumours suggested they had bought the people's loyalty by offering them bribes in the form of property and land.

The church had some odd practices—during a worship service, two young boys who looked terrified were dragged to the front and effectively forced to recite something akin to the "Sinner's Prayer." They were told that they had become Christians and the whole church praised God. Then, the pastor cancelled the church anniversary celebration at short notice. Apparently, the members had not done enough to bring visitors to the church within a specified time period. There was no regular Communion or partaking of the

Lord's Supper. The pastor, who was effectively unaccountable as he had no elders, decided when and if it was celebrated and the last one had been six months ago.

I accompanied the church leaders to a local meeting of all of the Bible Baptist churches in the area. During the main meeting, there were people calling out during the preaching, stamping on the floor, holding their Bibles in the air and bashing them in raucous agreement. A young man kept shouting "Amen, brother, that's right" and "Preach it." He was being parroted by a child each time he shouted. I didn't understand how anyone could concentrate on anything that was being said. I found it perversely amusing that, in the noisy environment, the women were wearing head coverings.

Then, there was the drama. The young people acted out a number of scenarios during which the Gospel was shared with different people and they either accepted or rejected the message. Some chose not to share giving various excuses. I was impressed, this was my kind of thing. But then, they switched to scenes of hell with victims languishing in regret and burning in the fire. The victims screamed at those who could have witnessed to them blaming their failures for the terrible punishment rather than their own sin. I found myself in a position I had never been in before, wondering whether there had been too much emphasis on judgement and not enough on grace.

During the fellowship meal afterwards, I was offered as a potential future spouse to a few of the young men whose fathers were pastors in the churches that had gathered. I thought they were joking until they began making height comparisons and on discovering that I was quite tall, one of the pastors solemnly informed me that he "had a taller son at home."

The Bible Baptist parallel universe aside, it was with a heavy heart that after a little less than a month, I reached the point where I knew I couldn't continue with this church. I felt sorry for the pastor and wanted in some ways to be the shining light that he had hoped for, but there were just too many areas of theological and practical difference.

I also had concerns about the second church I attended in Olongapo. The people's hearts were in the right place but they didn't know how to say "no." The leaders were run ragged and new ministries were popping up all over the place without the resources to sustain them. Their church building had recently been flooded yet they had an ambitious plan to create a shiny new community building for sport and ministry. There was a huge pledge board with the names of members and how much they had given to the project prominently displayed at the entrance to the church. When some of my "rugby boys" families attended the church, they were persuaded to take Communion despite not being Christians. Adding my "rugby boys" ministry to their ever-increasing list of activities didn't work in theory, or in practice as it turned out.

Then, there was the fun at immigration when the pastor had accompanied me to petition for a missionary VISA. The officials were rude to both of us. They didn't believe the pastor was a real one as they had never heard of his church. They demanded photos of myself carrying out "missionary work," whatever that meant. They suggested that I should switch to a church that was part of a recognised denomination. The lawyer was toying with us—one minute seemingly about to approve the paperwork and the next indicating he wanted to reject it. I don't know what harm he thought I was going to do to his country but he certainly created a dramatic scene out of what should have been a straight-forward matter. It was only afterwards that I realised he had been waiting for a bribe. After several months, my VISA was eventually declined, I lost two hundred pounds and was forced to begin the entire process again. Bureaucracy at its best.

I had intended to remain in Olongapo long-term, so the sudden necessary change of direction was difficult. I knew there was no such thing as a perfect church with perfect people but I also had to be willing to draw lines. The doors had closed in dramatic fashion and I was forced to recognise this. I wasn't ready to give up what I was convinced God was calling me to do. When the door to Cubao in Manila opened, I moved forward cautiously whilst desperately hoping and praying for a better church situation. I have learned (and am still learning), along with Elliot and many other missionaries, that God's ways are not my ways and His thoughts are not my thoughts. That there is a purpose in everything that happens and that success cannot be measured in human terms or on a worldly scale. That a life may be sacrificed to save other lives and that even in death God can be glorified.

I had cause to reflect on these truths anew when in February 2016 after a little less than two years serving in Manila, due to reasons beyond my control, I was again packing my things and leaving the Philippines not knowing if or when I would return. I had enjoyed my brief period of service in a country which in many ways already felt like home.

The question you no doubt would like the answer to is whether or not it is really "more fun in the Philippines." The Filipino's think so, the phrase has become the Filipino Department of Tourism's official slogan. I will reserve judgement for now and let you decide for yourselves as you read some of my experiences—the amusing, frustrating, confusing, exciting and mundane are all included for your evaluation.

CHAPTER ONE

House Hunting in a Hurry

House hunting isn't much fun at the best of times. Imagine doing it on foot, in a foreign country with an unfamiliar language, with approximately eight hours in which you *must* find somewhere, other than the street, to live, and all without the aid of the internet. This was the situation that faced me when I arrived in Manila for my apartment search. If it hadn't been for Chona, my Filipino friend, I would definitely have been hunkering down with the homeless people for the night. Maybe that would have been good for me. It's funny that our Western attempts to "experience" homelessness are always carried out under controlled conditions—we do it in groups and still have food, bedding and extra clothing not to mention the numerous gadgets. Of course, there are also the multiple risk assessments and safety aspects that have to be considered for a "worst case scenario." The homeless people just call it life.

We at least had a specific search area that limited our options—Cubao Reformed Baptist Church (CRBC) was in the centre of Cubao and I needed to be nearby. I was aiming for walking distance, not fancying driving in Manila which had few rules and consequently one of the largest road death rates in the world. We traipsed up and down the streets keeping our eyes open for crude, hastily written signs posted in wooden shack or tin roofed windows. They usually read "bed spacer"—essentially a bed in a dormitory, at least I hoped that was what the sign meant, rather than a space in a double bed! Other, less frequent signs were scrawled with "room for rent."

Ideally, I wanted to find a small house so that at some stage I could take in lodgers for company and cultural immersion. However,

I hadn't realised that the minute potential vendors saw me or even heard my voice on the phone, the prices would rise exponentially. I took to hiding around the corner or in doorways as Chona did the haggling, emerging swiftly with cash in hand to back up her assertions. The cautious owners looked Chona dubiously up and down, no doubt wondering what type of illegal activity she was involved in to be able to afford their rates.

Just as I was giving up hope—one place didn't have any light at all, the entrance was via a garage with men constantly working and there were large dead cockroaches on display in most of the rooms—we found a brightly coloured three bed-roomed town-house. It was in a private, gated road and just minutes from the church. I had ventured to enquire about the price knowing that it would be substantially higher than I wanted to pay, but realising that the alternatives didn't bear thinking about. The price wasn't too bad—fifteen thousand pesos a month (just over two hundred pounds which is about a quarter of what one would expect to pay for the equivalent in England.) The rooms were large, light and airy and, contrasted with everything else we had seen, it seemed like a palace. I didn't dwell on the fact that it was somewhat hedged in by the neighbours on three sides, or that it was in a flood plain. I hesitated for only a few seconds before requesting a meeting with the owner.

The Filipino owner, a man in his mid-30's, appeared flushed and somewhat anxious on his arrival several hours later. I wondered whether the price would mysteriously increase when he saw that I was a foreigner. To his credit, he confirmed the price as per the phone discussion with Chona, but he did inform me that I would have to pay *his* landlord fees for membership of a local association which I found a little odd. He raised his eyebrows when he discovered I was an evangelical Christian (rather than a Catholic,) as he started worrying about us turning the house into a church with loud worship meetings and upsetting all the neighbours. I assured him that as my actual church was within walking distance there would be no need for me to do this which seemed to calm him somewhat.

As it turned out, the neighbours themselves were pretty noisy. We were forced to endure early morning Tagalog singing and hearty laundry washing. Any and all private conversations sounded like they were in my room due to the open windows and close proximity. Shutting the windows was an impossibility in the summer if we wanted to stay alive due to the thirty-five sometimes forty-degree heat. I avoided using aircon due to the cost and not wanting to become reliant on it for the future. But, I lived in fear of electricity blackouts with the resultant halt of the necessary electric fans dotted around and running twenty-four-seven.

I was startled from sleep more than once fearing a man was present in my room and speaking to me when it was actually in a bedroom in the house next-door. This not to mention the teenager who decided that midnight was a good time to practice on his newly acquired guitar. There's nothing like getting to know the neighbours.

When it rained, which it frequently did, it sounded like the place might collapse as the water hammered on the roof with a deafening sound that made it impossible to sleep. In response, we ran around closing the shutter windows and occasionally checking the water levels and drains outside. Rain in the Philippines isn't comparable to anything you might see in England. Unaccustomed to such weather, I refused at first to even buy an umbrella insisting that I liked the odd rain shower. However, umbrellas are considered an essential item and I gave up in the end after getting soaked a few times. More importantly, I was fed up of explaining to people why I didn't have one and thought it was easier just to buy one to keep the locals happy.

Back to the landlord, I established later that the reason for the poor man's anxiety and initially hesitancy was that he had been plagued with problem tenants. They had virtually destroyed the interior of the house before leaving without paying the rent, and he had just finished repairing the damage. The contract had therefore been prepared with these issues in mind. There were a few anomalies to my Western mind-set—the tenant had to pay all the court fees in the event of legal action, but as I wasn't sure if this was a cultural thing, I let it pass. I did query the clause which stated that I was responsible for the upkeep of any plants and foliage in the house, which didn't have a garden. I suggested that surely it was a matter for me if I chose to let greenery that *I* had purchased die. But again, in the grand scheme of things, not really a big deal, how would the landlord even find out that I had neglected my plants resulting in their early demise?

After a few minutes perusing the lengthy contract, I stumbled upon the big one which also explained how the landlord would know exactly what was going on in my house—a clause that allowed the owner to enter the premises at any time of the day or night and without notice! I tried not to allow my mouth to gape thinking that surely, I had misread that section of the contract. But there it was in black and white. I wondered how to begin to address something of this magnitude and was curious to know the reason why a seemingly genuine landlord would even want this kind of uncensored access to my private life. I decided direct with a touch of humour was the best approach and just asked him outright. I pointed out that it was a bit ridiculous for me to always have to be on alert in case he suddenly burst in and said "aha." His response amazed me, there had been no mistake.

He explained that it might be necessary for him to "catch me in the act" of some envisaged possible illegal activity hence the need for immediate and uncontrolled access. I countered that he should at least knock on arriving at the door—what if I was getting undressed or having a shower? Initially, to my astonishment, he refused, insisting on the provision. But, I stuck to my guns making it clear that I would walk away. After a lengthy discussion, the contract was eventually amended to allow for my privacy.

Later, I relayed the discussion to some Filipino friends and was relieved that they were as shocked as I had been by the clause. Clearly, it wasn't cultural, just an over-enthusiastic landlord overcoming his past tenanting woes by attempting to become an amateur detective. What did I learn?—always read the small print!

CHAPTER TWO

Finding a Table

House rental contract signed, it wasn't long before moving day arrived. The four-hour journey from Olongapo to Manila in the front of a small truck squashed between the driver and his son was a new experience. We frequently hit bumps in the road at speed and I was forced to listen to the sound of my precariously balanced possessions being thrown around in the back. They had been packed Filipino style as I had cringed and bit my tongue nearby. I was amazed, and pleased, therefore to discover that a single glass was the only physical casualty on arrival, my nerves were shredded but they would recover.

Moving from an apartment to a three-bedroomed house meant that I now needed some additional furniture. Cash in hand, well, in my purse, I set out to find a small table or desk to allow me to use my laptop more effectively. I had been lying on my bed and awkwardly typing with it to one side of me on a cooler pad. The alternative was resting it on my stomach which almost burnt a hole through my clothes due to the machine being old and the battery getting extremely hot. I could've done with a replacement, but being frugal even before I became a missionary, I was determined to get every last ounce of usefulness out of every item I owned. It had become something of a game—see how long I can make this last before it falls to pieces.

The downside to this approach was definitely when things met the end of their useful life in public. My flipflops, that I was insisting on wearing until they had holes in the bottom, broke one day in the most inconvenient manner. I was in the middle of crossing a busy road with bags of food shopping and lots of people around. I fell into the road with all of my shopping and a small scream surprising the guy next to me who didn't attempt to help. Picking myself up from my undignified sprawl and pretending I hadn't hurt my ankle and knee, I hastily retrieved my wandering groceries. I then had to walk through the town and mall wearing one flipflop and carrying the broken one, until I came upon a shoe shop. However, I sadly traipsed out of the shop a short time later still carrying the lonely, broken shoe, having not bought a replacement pair because there was nothing cheap enough. The staff at the shop where I finally made a purchase had a good laugh at my expense as they gladly ditched the lone piece of broken rubber that had formally been my footwear.

Fortunately, I was now wearing more sturdy footwear as I set out with purpose to the only second hand furniture store in the area to hunt down my table. I was disappointed to find that the only slight, but not especially enticing possibility, was a heavily marked basic square wooden table with the price label inconveniently, and probably deliberately, obscured. It was standing forlornly outside the store in the middle of a lot of other junk that looked like it was waiting to be collected for immediate disposal. I knew that all the items would be useful to someone though and this appealed to my natural dislike of wastefulness. I asked the heavily armed guard at the door for the price as he seemed to be the only person around. Looking embarrassed at having been addressed by a white foreigner, which amused me because he was carrying a gun, he sheepishly turned and summoned a shop assistant from within the store. She in turn asked another assistant, or maybe the manager, who looked me up and down before announcing confidently "four thousand," about fifty-six pounds!

Appalled at their collective attempts to rip me off, I made it clear that the price was not acceptable, in a polite Filipino way of course with lots of smiles and laughter to cover up the gritted teeth and flashing eyes. When no immediate attempts were made to correct the error, I spun around intending to leave the store. At this point, the first shop assistant who had been standing dutifully nearby as I seemed to be the only customer, informed me that there were other items of furniture upstairs. I followed her lead up the rickety staircase into an upper room that was floor to ceiling with all manner of things. A narrow path had been created through the chaos although there wasn't any room to manoeuvre—wheelchair access wasn't even on their radar. I also dreaded to think how they would get anything out if I decided to buy something and was relieved that it wouldn't be my problem. It wasn't long before I spied some very nice desk tables all carrying the "four thousand" label. Clearly, the staff had been hoping to fetch the original price for their reject downstairs.

I wasn't really offended knowing as I did that it was part of living in a different culture. However, I was determined to get the best price that I could and not to walk away with a table that might fall to pieces after a few days or one that would be an eye sore. The lady staff member that had accompanied me upstairs finally conquered her shyness, found her tongue and then had a hundred questions. Maybe I was the only foreigner ever to have "graced" her store. Of course, my nationality and accent were the main topic, then my job and length of stay in the Philippines. She gigglingly complimented me on my language skills which I knew were basic at best. I was expecting to be asked if I was married and then why I wasn't married at my age, but she refrained.

Small talk in the Philippines is not the same as in England where we just say "How are you?" before walking off without listening to the answer or really caring what is said. The equivalent in the Philippines is "Where are you going?" After my attempts to politely explain exactly where I was going on a number of occasions, a local person finally informed me that I didn't need to tell strangers my schedule and that a vague reply of "just there" was perfectly acceptable. One man got a bit of a fright when I responded that I was heading for the church and that he was welcome to come with me. Well, what is an evangelist to do when given such a great opportunity?

I still wouldn't advise a visit to Manila if you value your privacy or feel uncomfortable when reading this. You may be forced to divulge uncomfortable personal details and may also be told that you have "got fat" at any point during your initial stay—this is a compliment as it is seen as a sign of good health!

Deciding against the haphazardly arranged tables largely due to the price as I was convinced I could do better, I thanked the curious assistant and left the store. I walked past the old "shoe man" sitting on the street next to a pillar in the same spot from morning till evening every day, he mended people's shoes for a small sum and they then returned to collect them later in the day. I did wonder whether those that used his services walked around barefoot for the day as most probably only owned one pair of shoes. The man was always very cheerful and I was pleased to see that he had a collection of at least fifteen pairs of shoes on the ground in front of him, sometimes it was just two or three. I often wondered how he managed to mend some of the shoes which really looked like they were on their very last legs. I also couldn't understand why people paid to get their broken shoes mended when there was a charity shop opening onto the street directly behind the "shoe man." I guess Filipinos were seriously attached to their shoes or maybe, like me, they just wanted to keep the dear old man in business.

Next, I walked past the heavily armed security guards outside various banks. Those that mustered the courage greeted me, "Hello Ma'm" with a smile and a nod making me feel a little like a VIP.

Arriving at a department store my bag was searched by another armed guard prior to entry. On finding a suitable new desk table for under twenty pounds I approached a check-out seeking to purchase it. There were a total of four lady check out assistants squashed into the booth which was only about one metre square. They were chatting to each other at high speed whilst customers waited patiently. I had learned that interrupting a social conversation, which for the girls was a higher priority than their work, would not be welcome. It was necessary instead to wait.

Finally, one of the assistants turned her attention to the lengthening queue and I was asked for identification in order to buy the item. The request seemed a little odd as I was paying in cash, but I'd learned not to argue with bureaucratic procedures that seemed to serve no obvious purpose, so I handed over my driving licence. I was issued with a claim form rather than a receipt—apparently, the salesman would double as the delivery driver later in the day and would swap the form for my receipt on delivery. Remembering my landlord lesson in relation to reading small print, I refused to sign the claim form which stated that I had "received the item in good condition." The salesman seemed bemused not understanding what the problem was—I was probably the only customer who had ever raised an issue with the form. He handed me the only copy of the unsigned claim form anyway. I then tried to pay for delivery but was informed that I could only do that when the item had been delivered.

Leaving the shop after what seemed like an eternity, I breathed a sigh of relief that I had accomplished my original goal with only low levels of bewilderment. Wandering back in the direction of my house, I observed a sign in a shop window which said something like "There are many beautiful and lovely things here for you to look at...But if you break it consider it sold." I mused that the English shopkeepers rhyme had been somewhat lost in translation.

I quickened my pace as I approached three working Filipino men. Nevertheless, they stopped what they were doing to stare at me before announcing "you are so beautiful," as I hurried away. Being beautiful in the Philippines doesn't have a lot to do with being beautiful. Another security guard smiled before raising his half-finished mug of coffee towards me and announcing "coffee" as I walked past his shop. I smiled and politely declined as I wasn't sure if he was trying to give me some of the coffee he was consuming or was offering to make me a fresh cup. It was pretty normal to be invited into people's houses when walking past and the first comment on entry was always "Let's eat!"

Clearly not paying enough attention to what I was doing, I was nearly ushered into a waiting jeepney by a conductor that somehow knew my first name. Jeepneys are the main form of public transportation, they are a smaller version of a bus but with no glass in the windows. It always amused me how locals seemed to allow themselves to be ushered into jeepneys even when they appeared to have had no intention of going in the direction that the jeepney was heading in. It was as if some were just wandering around without an intended destination and appreciated the conductor's acknowledgment that they existed.

I caught site of some street food that I took a fancy to although I had no idea what it was. Probably some form of rice cooked ten different ways as rice was the staple and served morning, noon and night. I bought a sample of each item from the very enthusiastic vendor and then gave him a Gospel tract which he took eagerly, instead of throwing it in the nearest bin like a Westerner!

I uneventfully passed the very quiet and subdued dogs that had on a previous occasion burst through a gate, that probably should have been locked, as I was passing. They had scared me and a few street children half to death by growling and snarling at us. Reaching the entrance to my new road, I acknowledged the only unarmed guard in the entire area by raising my eyebrows which was the normal greeting and then entered my house to await the hopefully imminent arrival of my new table.

CHAPTER THREE

Always be Prepared

Not long after my move to Cubao, my Filipino friend Arlene and I were walking along a main street. My attention was drawn to an approximately four-foot-high raised area which ran down the centre of the two-way carriageway separating the traffic. The road ran directly underneath and in the same direction as the Mass Rail Transit System (MRT,) creating a dark and gloomy atmosphere as the light to the underworld was blocked out. Often street beggars and homeless slept on the verges because they provided a good vantage point from which to beg at the windows of the jeepneys whilst they waited in traffic jams. The people could sleep off their substances, wake up, roll over, and with little effort or movement, immediately start begging for money from the temporarily trapped passengers squashed inside the jeepneys.

Being a light sleeper myself, I had no idea how people could sleep with all the very loud noises, not to mention the black grime that seemed to hover in the atmosphere. It ended up coating everything and everyone passing through and undoubtedly clogged the lungs of those choosing to sleep in the area.

On the verge, I could see two extremely dirty children crouching down and in the process of leaning in to a jeepney—someone was handing them a few coins from one of the windows. I watched the scene from the side of the road, fascinated and wondering who the children were and whether they were addicted to solvents, as many of the street children seemed to be. They were younger than the age that I had dealt with before. I didn't have to wait for long to find out more about them. There was a slight moment of jubilation as they examined the coins they had collected, then looking around they saw me and Arlene staring at them from the side of the road.

They immediately came running towards us, straight across the road which was more than a little worrying as they didn't even pause to check for vehicles. The older of the two children, a boy, led the way as the other hung slightly back, the leader had short dark hair and I guessed was aged about twelve. He was carrying a tatty rucksack that was bursting at the seams. The other child, a girl, looked about eight. They were both relatively thin and had black, tar-like, grime all over their clothes and smeared on their skin, it was especially evident on their faces. They held out their hands for money, but we wanted to find out a little more about them prior to giving handouts.

We established their names, Charlotte and Tracy, that they were sisters and that they were actually thirteen and ten. I managed to keep a check on my reaction to the revelation that they were both girls as the older definitely looked and was dressed like a boy. On my suggestion, Arlene convinced them to follow us to a nearby street food stand. I could tell that they weren't going to accompany us far from their original location as despite their initial confident approach, they had been suddenly overcome by an attack of shyness or possibly fear. After all, they didn't know who we were or what we were about or what we might ask them to do in return for feeding them.

We ordered some food from a brash Filipino lady and sat at the plastic tables and chairs next to the main street hoping that the girls would follow our example. We had unintentionally become the talk of the town, well at least the street, due to mingling with the despised and dirty street children. The girls may have been hesitant to accompany us, but an older street boy who happened to be passing had no such reservations. Realising that free food was available, Jason, fourteen, immediately accepted the offer to join us and began eagerly wolfing down the food that was placed in front of him. The older girl acknowledged him—they must have been at least a little acquainted. This wasn't that surprising as street children tended to end up as one big family supporting and looking out for each other, they all knew each other. Seeing that Jason wasn't afraid and was going to take what he could get; the girls finally joined us and ate some of the food.

I found that I couldn't take my eyes off the smaller child—she was wearing a tiny grey strappy top which on closer examination had originally been pink! I wondered how long it was since they had had a shower or cleaned their teeth or changed clothes. As I was with Arlene, I decided it wouldn't do any harm to offer the three children showers at my house. I didn't have any extra toiletries or clothes for them, but thought it might be a little helpful. Having established that we were relatively harmless, they agreed to the plan.

We walked the short distance back to my place with the children asking me every few seconds whether we were "nearly there yet." They took turns showering as I attempted in vain to get some of the dirt out of their clothes. I was pleased to see that Charlotte was carrying some spare clothes for herself and Tracy in the dirty worn rucksack, but the supposedly clean clothes smelled pretty bad. I tried not to cry as I wrung eight bowls of dirty water out of Tracy's tiny pink top, it was still filthy at the end of the process.

Meanwhile, there was a slightly unbelievable story emerging from the sisters that an adult had put Tracy in a sack, tied it up and thrown it in the river. Not knowing quite what to make of the allegation and still not knowing much about any of the children, I tried not to visibly react with the shock that I felt. Swayed by the emotion of the moment, I told the now clean children that they were welcome to visit for showers whenever they needed before inviting them to church that Sunday.

Myself and Arlene accompanied them back to the area where they had been begging, I was curious and wanted to see if I could work out where they had been sleeping. They disappeared under a grimy tarpaulin that was hanging at the entrance to an abandoned shop on the main high street. Looking in, the area looked more like a building site with many hazards but at least it was relatively sheltered from the unpredictable weather. Jason disappeared as soon as we hit the street, I figured he was probably involved in solvent abuse (a "rugby boy") and listening in on the girl's gossip sadly confirmed my suspicions. The sisters introduced me to another little girl with a cheerful smile. She was dressed in a short skimpy sparkling see-through bright purple dress and was sporting brightly painted nails and a pink hairband. It was only when she gave her name as Robert aged ten that I realised she was actually a he—a cross dressing ten-year-old! What would my extremely conservative church think about that?

CHAPTER FOUR

Rudely Awakened

I shouldn't have been that surprised to be woken by my very loud doorbell the following morning at some unearthly hour, I'm not a morning person. I hadn't even realised that I had a doorbell, so at first I groped around wondering where I was and in which country and whether there was some kind of an emergency. On re-joining the land of the living, albeit still in a foggy haze, I lumbered downstairs in my sleep-wear. Peering through a crack in the large metal gated door I recognised several of the children from the previous day who were gathering eagerly on the doorstep.

It was my own stupid fault as I had already forgotten a lesson that I should have learned during my dealings with the "rugby boys" in Olongapo; never give addresses or show the street children your house if you live in their hang-out vicinity. They are on the street twenty-four-seven with nothing to do but visit people who might be willing to give them time and attention. I had gone one step further than that and actually *invited* them to come—they must have thought Christmas had come early and I must have been having a mad moment, a lapse of judgement or some would call it naïve compassion.

Well, Charlotte, Tracy and Robert had responded to my invitation and there was nothing for it but to let them in. After their visit the previous day I had purchased some basic toiletries, towels and a few clothes in case they returned. They were very happy about their individually coloured toothbrushes and other items although I insisted that Robert could not have the pink one. Well, I had to start somewhere and encouraging Robert to consider whether he might be trapped in the wrong body was not on my agenda. I needed to find out why the children were behaving like this in the first instance, but I knew that it would take time.

The children's impromptu appearance, meant that I was alone at the house with them. The situation was less than ideal even in a place like the Philippines. Being female and a missionary helped, but I was still concerned about child protection issues especially as the children were showering. A family of church members were due to move in imminently which would put an end to any risk of allegations being made. Unfortunately, in the meantime, rumours started flying around the church that I had street children *living* with me. This obviously wasn't true, but I think it made the members wonder exactly what they had taken on in encouraging me to join their church.

Preventing the kids showering together or running in and out of the shower naked or exposing each other during their showers proved difficult at first. Robert enjoyed his showers so much that he sang loudly and enthusiastically throughout and although he had a sweet voice, I had to ask him to lower the volume because of the neighbours. Then, there had been a suspicious silence for a little too long so I reluctantly went and opened the door. Robert having finished his shower, was cheerfully washing his clothes in the tiny sink with a whole pack of bleach! He had filled the bowl to overflowing and was rapidly creating a mini bubble bath. I swiftly grabbed the bleach hoping to minimise the damage, but in the process got a minor electric shock from the socket that was dangerously positioned near the taps. I quickly ushered him out of the bathroom before removing all visible cleaning products to a high cupboard.

I determined to try to get to the bottom of the children's family backgrounds, but with my limited grasp of Tagalog and the children's' missed education this proved tricky. I decided to wait to try and address some of the issues at church with social workers from Christian Compassion Ministries (CCM.) CCM had been founded by my church and all the staff were required to be members, they operated children's homes as well as supporting children from slum communities in education via an Educational Assistance Programme (EAP.) They would surely know how to deal with the children and what local procedures were. I just had to make it to Sunday!

As expected the children turned up every day bright and early for their shower and basic food. I had tried to tell them they could only visit every other day so that I could sleep in sometimes, but they just looked confused and turned up every day regardless. I didn't have the heart to refuse them especially when it was wet outside and they turned up drenched and shivering. I did wonder whether their woeful appearances were a ploy though after catching them in the act of swimming in the gutters of the roads that had been flooded one day. A whole group of them were laughing, shouting and joking as fully clothed, they launched themselves into the filthy water and swam alongside the busy traffic. I didn't know whether to be horrified due to the very real dangers of disease and/or of being run over or pleased that they were getting some exercise and enjoying themselves.

Sunday duly arrived and all four of the children turned up at the church at different times, though none were on time for the children's Sunday school which is what they had been invited to. They each asked for me by name on arrival meaning that I couldn't disclaim them even if I had wanted to and I had to keep rushing out of the various services to welcome them. I was just happy that they had turned up. The situation had been less than ideal in the first place because usually I would have been able to tell them to attend the weekly homeless drop-in but it was closed for the two-month summer vacation.

The children were filthy and Charlotte and Robert had worn opposite gender clothes despite me having provided them with other clothes earlier in the week. I didn't think it would be too much of an issue as the church members would probably make the same mistake that I had initially made and not realise the reality. I decided to focus on getting through the day unscathed rather than worrying about such minor details. The adults when they did find out tended unhelpfully to giggle, gossip and state that Robert was behaving like that because "he's a gay," as if it were all a big joke. Charlotte was also labelled as gay due to her appearance and unfortunately shortly after I met Tracy she had had her hair cut short making her look more like a boy too. It was all very confusing.

Some members looked appalled and visibly disgusted by the dirty and unruly children. It amused me that they were torn between their allegiance to me as a white visitor and their natural rejection of the street life being brought into their midst. One or two of the leaders eventually ushered the children in, having initially hesitated and looked like they were unsure what to do. I wasn't going to allow the children to be turned away having made the effort to invite them, but I was concerned that it was not the ideal service for them. I sat in a row at the back of the church with the children all around me—two on each side

Of course, being a church that ran a homeless drop-in, there were a few homeless people that regularly attended the Sunday services. They tended to sit in a back corner and it always appeared a bit like they were separate from the rest of the congregation. I hadn't expected this—I had assumed that as the church members had a heart for the homeless they would already be integrated. The leaders later said they were working to improve the dynamics and, at the time of writing, more homeless people now attend the Sunday worship services. I also witnessed an element of voluntary segregation by the homeless people in terms of where they chose to sit—they preferred to lump together at the back where they could traipse in and out if necessary, have a quick snooze if things got boring and just generally remain unobserved by the smarter dressed majority. It was a lesson for me in first appearances being somewhat deceptive.

Sitting with and supervising the children in church was interesting. On each occasion they attended they took part in any one or all of the following activities at various points throughout the service; talked to each other loudly, passed notes to each other, passed notes to me and expected me to read them and respond, asked to go to the toilet and disappeared for thirty minutes, stared at people they knew and tried to get their attention, stared at people they didn't know and made comments about them, complained that they were cold and violently shivered to prove it, dropped pens, paper, hymn books and Bibles on the floor and then made a lot of noise recovering them, asked me who a person was and pointed at them, fell asleep, sang during the sermon, poked each other, poked me, stroked the hair on my arms, pinched my arms, pinched my hands, took the earphones of my translation device and refused to give them back, drew pictures of people in the church and labelled them, tried to sit on the floor, drew on the hymn books, pulled the plastic off the hymn books, stood up when they should be sitting down, sat down when they should be standing up, deliberately sang loudly and out of tune, crunched sweets that they had somehow acquired, put their feet on the chairs, kicked the chairs of the people around them, leant so far forward that their heads were touching their feet and stayed there until I wondered if they had fallen asleep. I think you get the picture.

By the end of every service I was totally exhausted having said "huwag" (don't) and "tahimik" (quiet) at least a hundred times and in the main been ignored. I looked up at the roof of the church as if I might find refuge there and breathed a silent prayer of thanks when it was all over for another week. I barely heard a word of the sermon.

Afterwards, there was a time of fellowship when the church members ate lunch together. I tended to join the homeless people's table so I added the street children to the motley throng. They ran around and began fighting with each other to the extent that one of the men in the church had to intervene to separate them. They settled down after a while but I did wonder what the future of it all was and was hoping someone that worked with CCM would suggest something. Unfortunately, it seemed that because their family was living outside Cubao there wasn't much that could be done for them. CCM needed to focus their resources on families living in Cubao.

A deacon approached me after the first service and asked what my plan was for the children. He said we couldn't have them running around the building as the insurance wouldn't cover it if something happened to them. I didn't really have a plan for them, I just wanted to bring them to church to hear the Word of God and hopefully get them some more support. My ultimate goal was to get them off the street and back to school but that was going to take more time. I realised that if I wanted anything to be done for this family, initially I was probably going to need to do it myself.

CHAPTER FIVE

Too Much to Handle?

I had been glad in some ways, that Jason hadn't chosen to join the others in turning up at my house on a daily basis—he was a "rugby boy," a little older and definitely more streetwise. But, of course, the day arrived when he showed up alone asking for a shower. I should've just said "no," but hindsight is a wonderful thing—during the visit he stole my cell-phone! My phone was cheap but the inconvenience of losing all of my contacts and the breach of trust was a painful reminder from my past dealings with "rugby boys." I heard on the grapevine that he had sold the phone for a pound or so. It had been a quick bit of cash for him but he had lost the chance of a shower, free food and the opportunity to hear more about Jesus having only been to church once. I hoped that he would remember that we had been kind to him if our paths should cross again.

Needing a more permanent arrangement for Charlotte and Tracy and wanting to get them off the street, I convinced them to let me visit their family home. Their mother, step-father and older siblings lived about an hour away from Cubao by public transport. The girls hadn't been to school for a number of years. I wanted to try and get to the bottom of whatever was going on at home and why the children had run away in the first place. They said there was no food there and implied that their mother had sent them to beg in Cubao to supplement the family income. They also hated their step-father, and although I couldn't ascertain the reason, the strong words used to express their negative feelings bothered me, particularly in Charlotte's case.

The four of us (including Robert) headed off after church one Sunday. Taking a jeepney for over half an hour and a tricycle with side cart up a steep hill, we arrived at the end of a long country track. The track had a steep drop down into a valley on one side and a comparatively shallow embankment on the other. Walking along the path, I was surprised to see wooden shack houses at different elevations on both sides of the track. I wondered how it was possible to live at such awkward angles, surely it would feel as if your house might suddenly lose its balance, and what about the rainy season?

The girls greeted those living in the houses who emerged as we progressed along the path. The people were keen to see a foreigner but not brave enough to speak to me. After some time, the girls indicated that we had reached their dwelling. I looked around but couldn't see anything resembling somewhere to live. Charlotte then veered sharply to her left, my eyes widened as I had thought we were walking along the edge of a precipice. Then, relieved, I noticed a very rough mud track that disappeared down the ravine-like drop. I followed Charlotte wondering what on earth I would find. Having pledged to try and help the children, I was now concerned about the possibility of being confronted with little more than a crudely constructed children's den in the middle of the undergrowth.

We arrived at something that would be barely more than a campsite by Western standards. A man, presumably the children's step-father, was cooking on an outside grill. There were chickens and fighting cockerels wandering around and a small wooden structure with a tin roof which was open to the elements on one side. The structure which probably measured a few metres in length, was divided into two. There was a board about three feet high with some bedding on it on one side, and a small television and a few other articles on the other. It obviously served as the family's sleeping and living quarters. The family were "blessed" to have access to a hose for their water supply.

A middle-aged, quite large lady appeared accompanied by a girl in her late teens who was carrying a baby. The children ran and hugged the older lady who I assumed was their mother. I was introduced to Diane, the mother and her oldest daughter Shelly, an unmarried teen mum. They all shared the tiny living space with the unemployed step-father who was doing the cooking.

Diane had made a special trip home for my visit, she was employed as a live-in helper for a family some distance away earning just three thousand pesos a month (about fifty pounds.) She only returned once every two weeks on a Sunday to see her own family which was, by all appearances, falling apart in her absence. In the past, Diane had been selling food locally to make a living, but her husband had lost his job as a construction worker forcing her to look for better pay.

It emerged that the step-father and an older brother had been involved in the "sack in the river" incident which they now claimed was a joke. I tried to make them see that the matter had traumatised Tracy, but it was difficult as Filipino's tend to have a somewhat different, we might say "dark" sense of humour and very different standards of child discipline. A Filipino friend of mine told me she had locked a child in a dark cubicle as a punishment knowing the child was afraid of the dark when she had lost her temper. I managed to hide my shock as I thought back to my child protection days and I imagined locking my friend up in a police cell for child cruelty offences.

I knew that the children would not stay at "home" unless their mother was there. I convinced her to quit her carer job and return to her home-made-food making business promising to subsidise the family's expenses and pay for the children's schooling. I shared the Gospel and gave them a Bible. We arranged for the children to stay at my house every Saturday night as a reward for good school attendance during the week and so that they could attend church on Sunday mornings. Diane also agreed to come to the church for the services once a month to collect the sponsorship money from me. She even agreed to look after Robert on a temporary basis because he refused to return to his aunt who allegedly beat him. Everything seemed to be straight-forward, but I knew that things rarely worked out as anticipated. God had a plan for the family though and I was praying for them.

I had been perhaps hasty in offering my Saturday evenings to the children, but I was just relieved that they wouldn't be turning up on my doorstep at some unearthly hour every-morning and that they would be back at school. The children were meant to arrive at 6pm but they were always early, sometimes *very* early. It depended on what type of mood I was in and my other commitments as to whether I was gracious and let them in or told them to go away and come back later. I did worry that if I sent them away they might end up in the company of the local "rugby children" for a few hours and that I would be at least partially responsible for any subsequent addiction.

They arrived at 2pm one Saturday and were told by my housemate to come back at 6. I could hear them downstairs again at 4 so took pity on them and made my way downstairs. I just about managed to hide my dismay that Robert was wearing a very pretty, long girls top with black leggings that had bows on them. By this point, I found that even I was getting confused about his gender as the way he dressed and behaved was so much like a girl. So, I decided to give up and hope that it was just a phase.

I took them to eat at Jollibee (the Philippine version of McDonald's.) En route, they cheerfully hung onto my arms as I complained that it was too hot and that they were exhausting me. My polite requests falling on deaf ears, eventually, I grabbed one of their arms and hung onto it pulling the child virtually to the ground to show them how hard it was to walk like that. Of course, they thought my over-reaction was hilarious, but my objective was temporarily achieved as they backed off.

Another child met us on the way and knowing that I found it difficult to say "no", the children invited him to join us without regard to who would foot the bill. My only question to the child was whether or not he was alone, I anticipated hosting another twenty children who would suddenly emerge from nearby streets at the offer of free food. Exaggeration? No, it had happened to me before. The lone child confirmed his solo status, so we continued at a more hurried pace to avoid being seen and ambushed by others in the area.

Arriving, the children disappeared whilst I was in the line. Looking around I saw that they were chatting animatedly with two heavily pierced and tattooed, rough looking men seated nearby. Cautiously approaching, I was introduced to the children's "close friends" who they had met whilst sleeping on the street. I nodded politely before ushering the children away from the dangerous looking men who had formed some sort of dubious attachment to the two young girls.

After eating, the Jollibee guard politely thanked us for coming, although I was sure he really wanted to thank us for leaving, as I removed the noisy party back onto the street. More children emerged, and I was forced to refuse their requests to accompany us. I always found it difficult, but had learnt that I couldn't help everyone at once and that it was better just to focus on one person at a time, or in this case four!

Continuing our journey, there was suddenly a loud clamour of adult male voices as at least three men gestured to me that they would like to finish the remains of the ice cream sundae that I was carrying. I felt slightly embarrassed for them—they were adults wearing nice clothes and shoes, not children and not homeless. I actually wanted my ice cream, so I ignored their requests and moved on.

Next, we had to pass a larger group of men in the street, I braced myself, knowing what was coming. One older man with hardly any teeth and a big grin declared "you are so pretty, I love you!" in my general direction. Before I could stop them, the children replied on my behalf, "She hates you and thinks you are ugly!" I shushed them and told them not to be so rude as telling someone you hate them is really very offensive in the Philippines.

We arrived safely back at the house and the children immediately began bouncing on my spare mattress that had been set up for them to sleep on in the lounge downstairs. They then set it on its side with one child balancing precariously on the edge of it whilst another rocked it back and forth. Maybe it hadn't been such a good idea to show them this particular game which they now insisted on playing every week. The children had become more confident as they got used to me and therefore more unruly and naughty. I made the mistake one Saturday of playing rough and tumble with them so having seen what I was capable of, from that date on, they expected the same. If I refused they tried to lure me into being drawn into the craziness. One weekend, they settled for me accompanying them outside with a skipping rope after Robert began a game that was "definitely going to break something" in the lounge! To the delight of my neighbours who had gathered to watch, I was then persuaded to take my turn at solo and group skipping something that I hadn't done and didn't plan to do again for a very long time.

The children became increasingly hyper-active and concluded the evening's entertainment by turning themselves into some sort of body ball which hurtled at full speed into our very firm wooden lounge table. Unfortunately, Tracy's head took the impact taking a chunk out of both object and child. The crack was really very loud but thankfully, although there was a lot of blood and I think an element of shock, all was okay in the end.

The children's favourite memories will probably relate to the time when our house had been overcome by mice. We tried sticky glue traps at first but they were a definite failure. They just resulted in a tiny mouse the size of my thumb getting stuck and writhing pathetically in the glue. I felt disproportionately sorry for the poor creature whilst realising that his minute size meant that we were now dealing with a mouse family as opposed to a lone ranger. This was *not* a joyous occasion for our household. Some evenings we watched the mice retrieving the cheese from the middle of the glue traps by carefully balancing on the edge of them. Those that were foolish enough to step in the glue just dragged the traps around until they bumped into something then used the leverage to free themselves. The final result was hundreds of tiny black paw prints all around the edges of the traps, but no casualties.

The children, distracted from watching a movie by sudden rapid movement in the kitchen, and my shrieking, tried catching the mice with their hands. Hands having failed, one of the kids picked up two traps and wore them like gloves intending to catch the mouse in the middle of the glue. Then another one got a kitchen strainer hoping to trap one like a spider underneath. The children, their excitement growing by the second, moved the fridge behind which the mice were by now eating my cheese. They came scurrying out at top speed, dashing around trying to avoid crashing into the children who continued chasing them. We witnessed some impressive acrobatics from the mice as they jumped and ran in all directions as they tried to get away. Needless to say, none of the children's efforts were effective and the mice went into hiding once again.

Mouse drama over for the time being, I managed to settle the kids down to watch *Finding Nemo*. Our internet connection was somewhat temperamental—we discovered that if one of the children sat behind the screen in a certain place on the mattress it worked okay, but that child then couldn't watch the film. We used a stack of pillows, which did the trick for half of the movie but then the whole thing crashed as we surpassed our daily bandwidth limit so I advised the children it was time to go to bed.

There was always additional chaos at bedtime because the children were afraid of various TV characters from films they definitely shouldn't have been watching. Chuckie and scary clowns loomed large in their minds and they often talked about the possibility of one or other of these fantasy creatures attacking them at night. I promised them that Jesus wouldn't allow them to be harmed in our home and that they didn't need to be afraid.

As for the mice, after testing a large rat trap which we couldn't work out how to set, and after a few people nearly lost their fingers, somehow the cheese disappeared again. We decided to reward the mice for their innovation and determination to stay alive by temporarily granting them a stay of execution and allowing them to live harmoniously in our midst.

CHAPTER SIX

He Has a Wife Already!

We persevered with the Saturday and church arrangement for the next two years with occasional blips as the children, and unfortunately at times their mother tested the boundaries. Diane at various points returned to her outside the home carer job which always resulted in the children returning to the street. I repeatedly banned them from staying over on Saturdays if I learned they had either skipped school or slept on the street for a night. I'm sure there were a number of times when it happened and I just didn't hear about it. I relied on reports from the locals who knew about the arrangements and delighted in reporting the children's misdemeanours to me.

There was also the sad night when I was heading back from a church fellowship with a group of friends. I came across a figure lying asleep in the centre of the pavement directly in my path. I had no idea who it was at first, or even whether it was a child or an adult, as the person was wearing a hoody obscuring their face. Wanting to check the welfare of the person, whoever it was, I stooped down to talk to them. I took a sharp intake of breath when I recognised Charlotte. She hadn't chosen the best location to fall asleep. In fact, she had probably inadvertently picked the most dangerous spot in the whole area. She was lying directly outside a building selling rooms and various unsavoury services by the hour. Probably the only reason she hadn't already been hired or lured away is because she was dressed like a teenage boy. She was still just fourteen.

With the assistance of some of my friends, I spent several minutes waking her up which was no easy task. We then helped her up and putting my arm around her shoulder, I led her back to my place for the night. I temporarily broke my rule about only allowing the children to stay over as a reward for school attendance and for *not* sleeping on the street. There was no way I was leaving her there, not only were the potential consequences unthinkable but there was also a strong typhoon approaching. My heart ached for her as I still hadn't been able to really get to the bottom of her troubles, but she was starting to open up a little and I was hopeful.

The following day, I gave her another clean set of clothes, including footwear which had mysteriously disappeared since our last rendezvous. I normally gave the children clothes that I had outgrown, which amounted to at least a few items every week. It was not because I was growing at the speed of a teenager, but because our local laundry shop kept shrinking them despite my plea to use a cooler wash. At least I knew they couldn't sell the clothes as the "rugby boys" in Olongapo had done—these clothes wouldn't be worth anything!

Several months after this incident, I again saw Charlotte in the street late at night. She was with some children that I recognised as having been involved in solvent abuse. When she saw me, she began racing back and forth across the road jumping in and out of the traffic and narrowly avoiding being hit by different vehicles that slammed their brakes on to avoid her. After hesitating and observing in horror for a few seconds, I left the scene as I knew that by watching her I was contributing to her desire to perform crazy and dangerous antics to an audience. I guessed that it was only a matter of time before one of the kids I was involved with was seriously injured or killed. I just kept praying it wouldn't happen and that God would keep them safe.

On the positive side, Charlotte and Tracy were by this point regularly in school and had become church and Sunday school attendees. They were also responsible for my "most embarrassing moment" which took place at my church. A white man that was married to a Filipino was visiting from England. Seeing him alone on the other side of the church, before I really knew what was happening, one of the kids suddenly grabbed my hand and dragged me across the room. I found myself awkwardly standing in front of this man and shaking hands with him as the child asked me loudly several times whether he was my "crush." I discreetly but firmly told the child "may asawa na siya" (he has a wife already.) I gave an embarrassed laugh and hoped the poor man didn't believe that I had put them up to it. The children saw two white people, a rare breed in the Philippines, and automatically thought they should be a couple.

Diane and some other family members also continue to attend the church at times and she even asked me for another Bible having given hers to a relative. She eventually separated from her husband due to allegations from the children. They effectively gave her an ultimatum—choose him or us. I had suspected for some time that Charlotte was dressing and acting like a boy as a form of self-protection from either her older brothers or her step-father. Her mother's long absences had made her an easy target and having worked in child protection as a former police officer, I recognised some of her behaviour.

The family situation made me sad knowing that the only true source of hope was found in Jesus. They couldn't yet see it for themselves and were grasping instead at straws. I had planted the seed and was desperately praying that God would open their eyes.

CHAPTER SEVEN

How's the Weather?

I had briefly returned to England due to ongoing illness. I had been a little disconcerted by the finality of some of the goodbyes on leaving and especially when one person thanked me for my "short term ministry in the Philippines." Either they had misunderstood my intentions, wanted to give me a very unsubtle hint or thought I would keel over and die prior to my return.

In the haste of my departure, I had no contingency plan when my bag containing nearly all of the clothing I possessed was lost en route. Of course, you are thinking that I could just wear the clothes I was travelling in for a few days. Foolishly, I had forgotten that it would be winter in England. Having shivered and complained for approximately fifteen hours on the aeroplane which didn't have blankets, I arrived in my flipflops, T-shirt and short trousers. I thought I might die of hypothermia when I stepped off the plane in London and discovered it was just four degrees! The following day, I had to go to church in a bizarre combination of clothes that were either too big, too small, unsuitable for the weather conditions or that belonged to other people.

My English doctor said that in addition to having an under-active thyroid, my vitamin D and iron levels were very low. He asked me how I was even functioning. I said that I wasn't hence my temporary exit from the mission field. After waiting in England for a few weeks, I made the controversial decision to return to the field despite not being completely recovered.

Thyroid issues are long term and will always have some sort of impact on a sufferer. Missionaries are not promised perfect health and in the past, they persisted with their calling despite sometimes being in serious pain or discomfort. I could either wallow in England or try and get on with the job and return home again if it became necessary. I increased my health insurance coverage though!

The day of my return to the Philippines duly arrived. I had a slight panic moment at security at Heathrow, London. Filipinos don't have access to a lot of Christian literature. This is partly because some believe that people who read are bookish or weird and partly because they tend to live for the moment. I wanted to make books available and so planned to gradually transport my personal library from England to Manila so that I could lend them to people.

Having jammed my carry-on bag with books, I was heading through security and had just been searched when I was asked to step to one side. A man who by dress and appearance appeared to be Muslim, approached me and pointed to my bag on the screen. There was a large, thick, block shaped object in the very bottom of it and he understandably wanted to know what it was. I thought it was a book but couldn't be certain. He indicated that I would have to empty all of the contents into a tray.

As I began the laborious process, avoiding eye contact as I pulled stray underwear and personal items out of my rucksack, I suddenly realised what the object was. I felt the colour rising in my cheeks and wondered whether I would make it to the Philippines after all as I finally reached the bottom of my bag and pulled out a brand-new copy of the large textbook entitled *Encountering the World of Islam*. I raised my eyes nervously to meet those of the man wondering whether he would be escorting me into a side office to discuss my inappropriate literature with members of the Counter Terrorist Unit. He looked vaguely amused and didn't bat an eyelid as he gestured that I could re-load my bag and continue on my way. I felt a bit foolish and resolved to pack more carefully in future.

Things weren't always so nerve wracking at Heathrow. On another occasion, I was slightly worried that I might be accused of smuggling commercial merchandise as I moved through security with a fair number of copies of my book *They're Rugby Boys, Don't You Know?* in my bag. My bag was again inspected, but this time, the staff member recognised me on the cover, became very excited as she read the back of it before exclaiming to her colleagues that I was an author involved in charity work abroad. She then handed copies round to all of them to read the back cover. Succumbing to speechlessness, I still had no words and was unable to correct her as she enthusiastically informed me I was a very good person and ushered me on my way.

CHAPTER EIGHT

The Kitten and the Cockroach

Arriving at my house in Manila, I met the stray ginger kitten that my housemates had acquired in my absence to try and deal with the ever-growing numbers of mice. I had seen photos of the animal on social media prior to my return and had thought it was cute. That was until I recognised some of *my* furniture in the background of the pictures and realised that the pet had actually been adopted into *my* household.

I'm more of a dog person, but my main concern was that the rental contract that *I* had signed specifically stated that we weren't allowed pets. I tried to reason with my housemates but they had already fallen in love, so I switched my attentions to the landlord, highlighting our rodent problem. Fortunately, he was amenable having by this point realised that we weren't out to destroy his livelihood as the previous people seemed determined to do. When I first saw the animal in the flesh, I thought it was a bit of a joke as it was so tiny I doubted it could catch anything. I was wrong.

Shortly after my return, I was in my room one evening when I heard a noise downstairs and went to investigate. I found Chiqui the kitten pouncing repeatedly on a medium sized cockroach. He was occasionally flicking it into the air and then waiting to assess its reaction. Of course, there was none as luckily for it, the creature that had now become Chiqui's latest toy, had long since passed on. I decided to leave them to the one-sided game of "tag" and went back upstairs. The next day I found pieces of black shell all over the lounge and was informed by my housemate that she had already cleared most of it up and that there had been not one but two victims.

It seemed Chiqui was of some use until he was big enough for the mice. He also became fond of doing normal cat things like bringing decapitated birds into the house then waiting expectantly, seeming to expect a reward of some kind for doing so.

Mice and birds, I could cope with, cockroaches I really couldn't. There were giant flying ones in Manila and on occasion I had awoken to find a large swelling on part of my body, usually my face. I was reliably informed that a cockroach must've bitten me during the night. A fairly large one had appeared in my bedroom one day. I had no idea where it came from. The revolting insect sat on the floor eyeing me warily as I looked at it in disgust. I hunted for a book to squash it. But, as the only option within easy reach without putting my feet on the floor and potentially in its path, was my Bible, I decided this wasn't appropriate. I also wondered if the horrible insect was too big to be squashed. I dreaded the sound and the mess. So, I instead spent twenty minutes trying to catch it with a broom and eventually succeeded in killing it. The bristles of my broom were as a result filled with mangled cockroach which wasn't pleasant but at least it was undoubtedly dead.

Predictably, Chiqui having been absent during this whole episode, made an early morning appearance a few days later when he was definitely *not* required. I had woken extremely early one morning for a trip to Olongapo when I was startled by a sound. I turned to see him bounding playfully into my room, probably having been sleeping just outside the bedrooms on a pile of boxes that he seemed to find comfortable. I groaned inwardly realising it would be a challenge to make Chiqui understand that I didn't have time to play and that he needed to be "very quiet." Sure enough, he started running around excitedly before lying on the floor watching me, then he pounced on my feet, making me jump several times. Next, like a child, he deliberately baited me by rolling towards the various wires plugged into the wall. I had stopped him playing with them earlier in the evening because part of his game involved chewing, the outcome of which might not have been pleasant. I decided to leave him to it, assuming he would get bored as children do, knowing I'd given him fair warning, and hoping he would find a different game before he electrocuted himself. "Goodbye Chiqui" I said firmly as I switched off the light and walked down the stairs. I headed straight out of the front door quickly shutting it behind me before my playmate attempted to follow.

Although Chiqui could sometimes be annoying, we all loved him really and were therefore quite upset when he went missing for about a week. By this point though, Chiqui wasn't the only animal living in our house as my housemates had added a ridiculously named puppy, Marshmallow to our number. I had returned home from visiting one day to find that the dog had taken up residence despite the rental contract stipulations. My housemates were acting as if they were completely unaware of the ban on pets and had obviously forgotten the fuss I had made about Chiqui. They were cooing over the puppy as if parting with him would be unthinkably traumatic. I realised I would be fighting a losing battle. Due to this addition, it was quite probable that Chiqui was feeling pushed out or a tad jealous.

Neighbourhood gossip suggested that he might have been "adopted" by other residents nearby. We especially noticed how quiet it was as he could get pretty noisy when hungry. He had also taken to fighting the neighbour's cat on most nights creating a serious disturbance as only cats can do. Then he vanished. We no doubt confused many ginger cats in the area during this period as we called out to them hoping for a positive response.

Eventually, I saw Chiqui a few streets away from our place. I recognised the distinctive collar and the loud meowing when he saw me. The meowing wasn't that friendly and he appeared to be hiding. A few days later I returned to the area with a housemate to try and recover him. There were workmen leaning on a cart nearby but no sign of Chiqui. I knew that Chiqui always responded loudly to his name being called so I suggested that we temporarily shelved our dignity. The men who obviously had no clue what we were doing seemed somewhat startled and maybe embarrassed on our behalf as we loudly called the elusive cat. Unable to tolerate the public humiliation for much longer we were in the process of giving up and leaving. It was then that I heard a faint meowing which had the distinctive, familiar Chiqui ring. We located him nearby as he continued meowing and my housemate managed to pick him up. Safely back and seemingly happy to be home and back to his usual antics, we wondered if he might just have been lost.

CHAPTER NINE

Language Learning

In-between the Charlotte and Tracy drama and the tales of Chiqui, the street kitten, I focused on learning Tagalog, the local language. My new church had an English service on Sunday afternoons which had been part of the appeal because I was struggling with no proper spiritual input due to not being able to understand the sermons in Tagalog. I knew that learning the language must be my main focus for my first few years if I really wanted to be able to build relationships and share the Gospel.

I have never had a particular aptitude for languages being the one who spoke French in my German class and vice versa for the entertainment of other students at school. I scraped a B in the end in my German exam but only because my teacher was giving me massive clues using her body language—changing herself into an aeroplane or screwing up her face when I headed in the wrong direction. I guess she *really, really* wanted her students to pass. Her final question was "What do you do on a typical day?" and as it happened, that was the only thing I had learnt over the course of five years.

I had begun learning lists of Tagalog words with Arlene and a basic phrasebook whilst still on the Logos Hope. I learned the essentials needed to tell the street children to do things, or more often *not* to do things. My first phrase was "sandali lang" which means "wait a moment," but I was even pronouncing that wrong. However, as I was quickly learning a lot of words I naively thought the rest would be easy. It doesn't help that saying even the most basic word to a Filipino in Tagalog always results in a ridiculously over the top amount of praise and comments like "You know Tagalog, you are very good." People always say that it is easier to learn a language when you are surrounded by it and immersed in the culture, I believed them.

The few lessons that I did have descended into hysterics as a result of my wrong translation of various words. Early mistakes included confusing the words "pusa" (cat) and "puso" (heart) thereby telling an audience that Jesus was living in my cat. I was also ridiculed by one of the street kids when I told him that he was "jealous" (inggit ka) instead of to "take care" (ingat ka.) I solemnly informed a teacher that "My coffee likes to drink me" before explaining to a group of children that I liked a cockroach eating my face, instead of that it was the cockroach who liked to bite my face. I also thought that a "cow" was going to do something "tomorrow" but the real meaning was that "maybe" the place was "open." I probably should have looked at the pictures in the book and realised that a cow had nothing to do with the story. I somehow told another teacher that I had stopped attending a church because the people there were too small which resulted in a bizarre discussion about the possibility of an elf or smurf church. Being a foreigner and tall in comparison with most Filipinos this mistake was of course hilarious. I had just said the words in the wrong order to achieve this unintended result.

But by far the biggest problem I had was that Filipinos expected me to speak English, so didn't listen for Tagalog, and therefore didn't understand it due to my accent. And that often they responded in English, because they wanted to learn English, or wanted to impress me, the foreigner. There were few that were willing to correct me. Those that did were reluctant to go into detail about my mistake preferring to gloss over it or seemed embarrassed and wished they hadn't said anything in the first place.

The headache really began the moment I started learning Tagalog grammar. There are twelve words for every verb and each time you use a different one of the words you also have to change all of the other words in the sentence. Tagalog doesn't just have past, present and future tenses but also a focus or emphasis within the sentence. The vast numbers of variations continue in every aspect of the language—there are eight different ways to say a person is very tall rather than the three in English. There is also an extra letter in the alphabet "ng" which is very hard for a Westerner to pronounce. I learned when singing in church that Filipinos also have a different sound for their "t's. It's amazing how loud that "t" is when no one else is singing it! My teacher told me to "swallow my t's" but I never quite figured out how to do that.

The funny thing (or annoying depending on your perspective) is that the Filipinos believe that English doesn't make any sense because of words like "cough" and "bow" and the other anomalies of the language. But from my perspective, the only easy thing about Tagalog is that most of the time the words are spelt as they sound. And, I couldn't for the life of me work out *why* there needed to be a particular focus in a sentence which definitely quadruples the number of words required and confusion rendered to a Westerner. "Aaah" the locals say "Tagalog is clever because as soon as you hear the verb you know what the focus of the sentence is." They start the sentence with the verb as well which is also the opposite to English. Honestly, knowing the focus of the sentence was the least of my worries when trying to work out the meaning of all of the other words, which order they went in, which time tense to use and where to use the tones and glottal stop!

The pastor of my church in Cubao is English but has lived in the Philippines for several decades. He speaks fluent Tagalog and kept reminding me that if I couldn't even pronounce the word Tagalog correctly then there was no hope for progress beyond that. One of my language teachers seriously misjudged my ability and mistakenly decided I had an aptitude for learning quickly. She sped through the lessons in whirlwind fashion. After six weeks of this, I was left dazed, confused and only a little further forward than when I had started. I was severely demotivated and it had reached the stage where I was dreading my lessons. I took a break, fearing a permanent scar and although I improved through general conversation, I never actually returned to full time language study.

I have been encouraged since that terrible time when I was feeling like a complete and utter failure by two unconnected people. They both said that Tagalog was one of the hardest languages they have ever seen and that it should be up there with Thai or Chinese. One missionary even said that he was daily praying for God to take him home during his lessons as he hated them so much!

CHAPTER TEN

Bureaucratic Nonsense

Those that have read *Planet Police,* another of my books, might recall this chapter title, and how irritated bureaucratic procedures make me. However, living in the Philippines made me grateful for my experiences in England which by comparison were plain sailing.

I wanted to upgrade the pocket WIFI at our house. The connection speeds via GLOBE (named and shamed) were consistently well below that advertised. But, whenever I contacted Globe online, which in the first place required sufficient signal that we often didn't have, I usually got cut off halfway through the online chat. I then had to go through the whole procedure again. Alternatively, I could email asking for the procedure for an upgrade, which usually resulted in a failure to answer my question and a request for twenty items of security information

Next on my list of bureaucratic nightmares are Filipino hospitals though I was blessed only to have to spend limited time in and around them for personal illness. Dealing with the homeless who always had various ailments and long term illnesses, however, resulted in frequent trips there. I accompanied a lady one day for an eye check-up, we arrived a little flustered having been given the wrong directions and heading out of town on the wrong jeepney before realising our mistake and returning. We were informed that it wasn't possible to get a check-up and to return at 7am the following day. I tried to look crestfallen and waited for a few seconds in the hope that the nurse would change her mind. This seemed to do the trick as she then agreed to admit us as an emergency case. After filling in some forms we waited and waited and waited. Eventually, the eye doctor diagnosed cataracts and arranged follow-up checks and eye drops. So far, almost good.

The ridiculousness only began after the procedures had finished and we needed to try and pay the very small bill and obtain a discharge notice. Remember this was for a simple eye problem and purely as an out-patient. We first had to collect some paperwork from one building, then go to another building to obtain our bill. We then stood in a queue of about thirty people to try and pay the bill until we were moved by a guard to yet another building to join a shorter queue also to try and pay the bill. Bill having been paid we had to return to the first building to show that the bill had been paid, then obtain a receipt. We then had to go to another counter to obtain a discharge notice and allow the security guard to check that we had been discharged before we could leave!

Whilst we were waiting at the final stage a very large and clearly ill, semi-conscious woman arrived at the entrance to the emergency department. She was balanced precariously across several seats of a tricycle as people rushed in all directions trying to work out what to do. Eventually the poor woman was bundled in a rather undignified manner onto a stretcher which appeared as the drama moved inside the doors of the already full hospital. Looking around inside I was appalled at the apparently serious conditions of many of the patients lying on stretchers awaiting attendance.

I was about to piously shake my head at the predicament and render judgement on the still developing nation, but was forced to check myself. I realised things were not much improved in England. The main differences are that the doors to the hospital would be closed preventing general viewing and that the ambulances would be queueing outside with the patients onboard until there was room enough in the corridors for them to be offloaded.

My final award for bureaucratic madness, well at least for now, goes to the Philippine central post office. I became so exasperated with the postal system that I stopped people sending me parcels from England. I always dreaded receiving that little card saying that a parcel was awaiting collection at the central post office because I knew that it would involve me taking an entire day out to travel to the office and that the parcel was accumulating storage fees in the meantime. The notice had usually expired by the time I received it and there were never any phone numbers or even an address on the card to tell me where to find the elusive collection place.

I once set off in the vague general direction thinking I would "ask someone" when I got closer. I should definitely have known better by this point as I had already been in the Philippines for a while. I knew from experience that I could ask four Filipinos and be confidently directed in four completely different directions. People didn't like telling me as a foreigner that they didn't know where something was and I guess my accent and resultant misunderstanding accounted for the rest of the mistakes. This occasion was no different and I found myself in the unfortunate position of having to weigh up the various conflicting pieces of information based on how "reliable" a person looked.

Eventually after travelling on the MRT for a few stops I found a jeepney to take me the rest of the way. The MRT which travels in a straight line along a track, is an interesting phenomenon as there are far more people trying to travel on it at all times of the day and night than can possibly fit, resulting in people being "bent" to fit inside. If you watch it from a distance you can often see peoples' faces and limbs literally squashed against the windows as about three times the safe number of people have piled into a carriage. Even more amusing is that usually the carriage next door is virtually empty as for some reason everyone has headed for the same one. One day the MRT overshot the last station heading out onto the street. Commuters and pedestrians rushed to see what had happened, most of them more concerned with taking "selfies" and posting them to Facebook than anything else. It was like they just couldn't believe that what had happened was even possible ad it was the talk of the town for weeks!

Anyway, so I ended up on a jeepney hoping that I was headed for the right place. I checked with the driver who abruptly told me to "wait." But, growing increasingly concerned, I began asking other passengers, thinking the driver's reluctance to converse meant that he didn't know. The passengers unfortunately asked the driver again.

He became understandably irritated muttering under his breath that I was "naughty." Clearly, he wasn't expecting me to understand until I responded "not really" in Tagalog and he looked very embarrassed. The kind old man, despite my cultural rudeness, did a detour from his prescribed route and dropped me right outside the post office. I felt obliged to tip him but couldn't find any change so gave him a hundred pesos (over one pound) which really made his day.

Entering the post office, I was not surprised to see far too many staff to deal with the very few customers. They couldn't find my parcel and one by one went searching for it before giving up and handing the matter over to someone else to continue. After fifteen minutes or so they located it and started completing a lot of, I'm sure unnecessary, paperwork before I could take it and leave. I asked the staff member if they delivered parcels due to the inconvenience, travelling and storage costs incurred. She advised me that they only delivered books. I knew that my parcel contained a book as it was clearly marked as such on the customs declaration. I pointed this out to her. She promised me that next time, they would ensure they delivered any books that might arrive for me. I was totally bemused by her response knowing that, with millions of customers, her promise was empty, unless she planned to devote herself full-time to the task of waiting for, and delivering any books that I might personally be expecting.

My post office fiasco was compounded as I opened my parcel on leaving and discovered a single book by John MacArthur entitled *Being a Dad Who Leads*. Very useful, I'm sure!

CHAPTER ELEVEN

The Fun Side

Socially, Filipino's enjoyed eating or drinking out, wandering around malls, and loud karaoke. A lot of them had aspirations to become famous singers—I heard some truly terrible efforts as well as some real talent. Indeed, one Bible student at my church had formerly appeared on the Filipino equivalent of *American Idol* or *X-Factor* and had gone on to win it. He said that there wasn't much to do when growing up so he just borrowed his neighbour's guitar and practiced and practiced. He then used his talent to teach others to sing hoping some would get a break and be able to use their voices to rise out of poverty.

Soon after my arrival in Manila, I somehow ended up accompanying some of my housemates to an open-air rock concert. I had thought I had said goodbye to this type of music when I became a Christian, but wasn't really aware of what I was going to until I was there. We were all seated at tables in front of the stage and waiting for the main band. The emcee was wandering around with a microphone obviously seeking a victim. I was hiding knowing it would be me as I was the only visible foreigner present. Sure enough, glancing around, he made a bee line for our table and asked me to stand up. I tried in vain to refuse the humiliation, but my friends thought it was a great idea to embarrass me and egged him on.

After a few mundane questions and having established that I was single, he asked me "What do you look for in a man?" I paused for a second, knowing I needed to be honest but wishing myself far away.

Missionary in Manila   57

"Well, he has to be a Christian, because I'm a Christian." There was an awkward silence, then some uncomfortable laughter from the man who no doubt regretted his subject choice. Then, the microphone was swiftly snatched away as I lamely concluded that my ideal man would also need to be "honest." My friends were impressed, I was mortified. It didn't bode well for me if I were to be threatened with serious persecution, I had been tempted to avoid the subject of faith altogether.

Most Filipino's don't have a pattern of regular exercise, although the men play basketball and there are a few who go out running. Swimming is popular and as with most things is seen as a group activity, but they don't actually swim, they just splash around. A lot of Filipino's can't swim which sadly explains the heightened death tolls after floods and tsunamis. I had thought of myself as relatively modest in comparison with my Western peers, but in the swimming pool most Christian Filipinos covered up and wore T-shirts and shorts or longer swim-wear. I began adopting this approach realising that Western swimming costumes are really akin to wandering around in public in one's underwear, and that's without mentioning bikinis!

We visited a spa and swim place for a day out. The main swimming area had a fast-flowing wave pool and a number of pressurised valves that could either be sat on or stood under. There was even a water massage, the idea being that you lay flat and were pummelled by a number of streams of water. This appealed slightly more than a traditional massage which I have always avoided. Massages are offered everywhere in the Philippines, a Bible student from my church even ended up leading a Bible study with ladies in a spa. Of course, he was offered a free massage on every occasion, but eyebrows were being raised at church and it was suggested that maybe it wasn't appropriate.

There was another area with four jacuzzi type structures. They all bubbled at different rates, had different smells and were kept at varying temperatures. I began to step into one before hastily withdrawing fearing second degree burns might result. I could tolerate one of the others for a few seconds. Incredibly there were actually people fully immersed in these temperatures although I'm not sure how much of their skin they retained. Not my idea of relaxation.

A few of us one day went ice-skating. The girls were really excited about it so I assumed they had been before and knew how to skate. But, it was actually their first time, so they spent the entire session clinging to the sides or wobbling along next to me and grabbing me every few steps as I also struggled to stay upright. I was at one point unexpectedly taken hold of and pulled causing me to go flying. A concerned looking instructor came rushing over to retrieve me from the undignified heap on the floor. As always, it was my pride that suffered the most as I looked around for someone to blame and found one of my friends sniggering and snapping photos at a safe distance. I thanked the safety guy and hastened to the nearest wall for refuge.

For the benefit of my Filipino friends and to assimilate into the culture, I was compelled to visit all of the local tourist attractions. This brought back memories of doing the rounds in Olongapo with my friend Penny from England during her visit the previous year. I had enjoyed the strange experience of being pecked to pieces by some tiny colourful birds that had arranged themselves all down one of my arms. When being photographed with a huge white Bengali tiger there was a lack of pre-planning resulting in terrified Penny sitting nearest to the tiger's head. The man automatically gave her the feeding bottle which she refused before she began loudly hyperventilating, definitely the wrong thing to do in the presence of a gigantic tiger! The fun didn't end there. Next, we queued and donned large red winter coats to enter a Christmas snow simulation. The Russians that we met inside were similarly unimpressed coming from one of the coldest countries in the world.

Returning to Cubao, when it was time for the real Christmas celebrations, things were quite subdued. A lot of Filipinos used the time off work to travel to see family members in the provinces. There were no church services due to the many people absent. People gathered together in houses and as always, there was a lot of food! We opened our house to some of the girls that lived in the children's homes run by CCM for one of the days. I felt quite homesick during this time due to usually being with my family.

New Year was completely different as people tended to flee the city to avoid the blanket smoke from the massive number of fireworks. I thought it was a joke when someone first advised me to leave, but they were deadly serious. The air could become so polluted that it was difficult to breathe. I chose to remain when my housemates went away and headed out onto the street with some church friends to check out the festivities. We joined a throng of people in the road next to our house who were watching the very dangerous and potentially lethal antics of a few crazy individuals who had somehow been put in charge of the fireworks. They set them off about a metre away from the onlookers with no safety precautions whatsoever. Fireworks exploded in all directions and I actually felt the remnants landing on me as the leftover pieces fell out of the sky. I obviously survived the experience which in some ways wasn't much different to my childhood in England. Due to the huge bonfire my dad erected for our church youth group each year, we had regular unexpected visits from the fire brigade.

CHAPTER TWELVE

The Criminal Underworld

Some say Manila is a dangerous place but it didn't *feel* dangerous, maybe I had been lulled into a false sense of security. Working amongst the street homeless and solvent addicts helped, they were always around and would probably have been the first to come to my aid if I had cause to summon them. There was a bag slashing trend making the rounds. The perpetrator approached an elderly victim with a long-bladed knife and, having made the quick incision, made off with any contents that fell out of the hole in the bag. I couldn't understand why the method yielded more than just grabbing the bag, but I'm sure there was a reason.

I was on a jeepney one day when the young lady next to me was robbed. It happened in broad daylight and in seconds before anyone really knew what was happening as the vehicle had temporarily paused. A young hooded male appeared at the entrance and roughly grabbed her Smartphone from her hands before walking nonchalantly away. There was no violence but only because the terrified woman had submitted to the inevitable.

Some jeepneys were privately owned or rented and there was little or no government regulation at least in terms of appearance, I hoped there were some minimal safety standards. Smoke billowed from modified exhausts choking passers-by. There were owners that covered their vehicles with crude paintings of evil faces and played loud thumping heavy metal with the artists screaming at the tops of their lungs. This contrasted with others that were decorated with Bible verses and pictures of Jesus. If you ended up on the former it was an endurance test both of patience and of safety as some of the drivers looked as if, in addition to the mad environment that they had created, they were also high on drugs.

I happened to board one of them in the evening one day with a friend. A man sitting near to the driver was staring at us and something wasn't right. When we paused to let some people alight, my friend grabbed my hand and told me in no uncertain terms that we were getting off immediately. I followed her lead and later she said that it hadn't been safe and she thought they had planned to take us somewhere or do something to us. Other than the bizarre jeepneys, the other visible sign that Cubao was a rough area were the numerous hotels with their hourly rates posted prominently outside in bright colours for all to see.

As a foreigner, I had been pre-warned about unethical taxi drivers. I had a couple of bad experiences. One was when I became ill when I was out of town one day. I desperately needed to get home as soon as possible as I could feel the blood pounding in my head as I was about to pass out in the heat. I had been trying to flag down a taxi for at least an hour but was competing with a line of other people who couldn't have cared less about my condition. I finally persuaded a driver to take me but he wouldn't leave until I had agreed to a price nearly four times the usual rate. He said it was due to the likely traffic, I didn't have the strength to argue with him as I collapsed in the back of his taxi and then had to instruct him to pull over after just a few minutes so that I could do the necessary out of the back door. Arriving home, my housemates were shocked by my appearance and furious when I told them what had happened.

The second incident was when I was heading to my least favourite place in the world, immigration. I had to go there every two months to renew my VISA and it was not an easy journey. A taxi driver was making what I thought was polite conversation or maybe testing his English, so I absent-mindedly answered him. I perked up when he asked me how much my VISA was going to cost and before I had really thought about the reason for this enquiry I had responded truthfully. Realising that he might now think that I was carrying the money somewhere on my person and that I had thus placed myself in danger. I clarified that I still needed to access the money and that I needed to be taken to an ATM. As I was saying this, I was carefully manoeuvring my purse and passport into more secure and less visible locations.

I didn't like the way the man was watching me in his rear-view mirror. He tried to get me to agree to pay a percentage of my VISA cost for his cab ride, something like two thousand pesos which was about ten times the going rate. Boldly, I told him to put the meter on straight away and that I would get out of the car if he failed to do so. He then tried to get me to agree to a hefty tip. Quaking inside and with a silent prayer, I told him calmly that the more he badgered me the less likely be would be to get a tip. There must have been something in my tone because after arguing with me for a while he did as he was told and dropped me off without further incident. I was relieved and grateful to reach my destination unharmed and learned to take public transport after this.

CHAPTER THIRTEEN

The City Awakens

I woke early one day, about 4am, otherwise known as stupid'o'clock in my "I am not a morning person" world. I was planning to head to Olongapo, my former city of residence. Honestly, my heart was still very much with the "rugby boys" many of whom had by this point been released from rehab in Manila and were back in Olongapo. I had been considering creating some sort of Christian institution or half-way house encompassing education, vocational training and if necessary a rehab. I hadn't worked out the details and it was still just an idea at this stage.

The senior pastor at my new church had suggested that if I wanted to continue working with the "rugby boys" I would need to find men to join in the work. He encouraged me to focus on ministry to girls. I was at first devastated by his advice knowing that I would need to submit to his authority and follow it but believing I had been called to the "rugby boys" ministry. It wasn't that I wanted to work with boys, it was just that most of the solvent addicts were boys, although in Manila girls were doing it too. After my initial emotional reaction, I recognised in my heart that he was probably right, the original boys were no longer ten to fourteen, most of them were mid to late teens and this made a difference.

My first priority was to get integrated in my new church, to help out with their ministry and then to try and get them on-board in helping me with the boys. My church leaders were aware of my desire to help the solvent addicted children and expressed an interest in becoming involved. I therefore visited Olongapo at regular intervals to maintain contact with the government youth centre and the boys living on the street, whilst I prayed for longer term solutions.

I headed towards the exit gate for my road. It was locked—I hoped not with a padlock as this would have involved some relatively undignified climbing. I fiddled with the chain to no avail and was in the process of wondering what to do next when our friendly neighbourhood guard approached me with a small towel around his shoulders. I wondered where he had emerged from as I could see only a wooden shack house on the pavement nearby. I hoped he hadn't been lying awake all night on tenterhooks just in case a crazy resident decided to leave at 4am and needed the gate unlocking. He greeted me cheerfully, a little too cheerfully. I wondered why the Cheshire grin until he reached the gate and gave it a very small push to emphasise that it was already open. We both laughed at my stupidity as I made good my escape and he returned, I assume, to his very un-satisfying sleep.

Heading into town, I discovered that the streets were already buzzing with activity as people began their daily routines. Unfortunately for many that involved rummaging through other people's garbage to salvage anything recyclable or edible. I noticed too that the street dogs that were usually partakers were asleep leaving the first pickings to the people, which kind-of made the situation even more poignant. Bizarrely, I found myself wondering why they weren't wearing gloves to protect themselves from the filth, before shaking my head at my non-sensical thought processes. Several people acknowledged me as others openly and curiously, without malice or unfriendliness, stared. A normal part of life that followed me everywhere I went due to being a rare foreigner on their turf.

A teenager greeted me cheerfully in perfect English as he cleaned out a plastic bowl in the street. There were signs everywhere advising people not to urinate. I wondered what the homeless people were meant to do. The government didn't provide facilities for them so what choice did they have? Even with this knowledge it was fairly disgusting walking through the streets and having to avoid any wet patches just in case, especially wearing flip flops, which were the standard footwear. It was also quite normal to see people in various stages of undress either because they had nowhere to get changed, because they were high on drink or substances and didn't care, or because they had no clothes. It was just another part of the undignified reality of living publicly on the street.

The rampant homelessness was also more evident at this time of day—numerous people sheltered under plastic umbrellas lying uncomfortably on flat cardboard boxes. Their children huddled next to them, the most recent victims of floods and typhoons. Some people slept alone; friendless, unwanted, unloved.

Then there was a mass of bodies with limbs all entangled on top of the raised areas in the centre of the street with noisy traffic flowing both ways just inches from their sleeping bodies. It was the equivalent of people parking themselves on a central reservation on a dual carriageway! I stared openly trying to work out whether they were adults or children, if it had been England I would have found it difficult to accept that they were real people due to the location, but in Manila anything goes. Finally, I realised it was the current hang-out for the solvent addicted teens who had probably collapsed into the pile whilst high the previous evening. Some were there as a result of rebellion as they had perfectly good homes to go to, but most were from families broken by abuse and poverty.

Sometimes, I wondered why people chose the main high street of Cubao with the twenty-four-hour traffic and high pollution levels. But I figured that there were other dangers in a more remote place and one dirty, dusty street was more or less the same as the next. I quickened my pace as the desire to gather them all off the street and into a proper shelter in any building anywhere, hit me, along with the realisation that the problem was overwhelming and that providing somewhere for them to sleep didn't address the root, not really. Living in Manila made me truly thank God every night for an actual bed to sleep in out of the weather conditions be they too hot, too rainy or too stormy as was so often the case in this part of the world.

A rough looking man walked towards me and I felt just a touch afraid as it was still pretty dark, until he brushed past me with the customary "Hello ma'am." He would've tipped his hat had he been wearing one and I was instantly reassured as thoughts of robbery or other violent crime vanished as quickly as they had come.

I walked over the very dark and dirty overpass unable to see even my feet in front of me and noticed a man ahead of me on the steps attempting to carry far too much. I thought about offering to help him but decided he would probably be embarrassed by the offer of help from a white foreign female. In any event, we headed in different directions at the top of the stairs. I narrowly avoided tripping over things and people setting up their stalls on the bridge, by following the path of the many others around. I wondered how people motivated themselves to get up at 4 or 5am to sell sweets for one peso (just over a penny) that they had purchased in a supermarket for half the price. There were already many such vendors around also selling individual cigarettes from an open packet. They had no choice if they wanted to feed their families.

I walked down the other side, then speeded up as I manoeuvred along the edge of the hundred-metre-long, two-metre-high railing separating the pavement from the road where the buses were. It was really irritating to see a bus going to the place I wanted to get to but not being able to catch it because the fence was in the way. Most people rushed to reach the end of the barrier so that if their bus happened to be passing they could risk their lives by jumping into the fast- flowing traffic and flagging it down. They could then buy a ticket on the bus and reach their destination more quickly. Sadly, it seemed that on this day, every destination was listed on the racing buses, apart from Olongapo. I was doomed once again to bus terminal bureaucracy. Hooray!

CHAPTER FOURTEEN

Speed, Safety and Suspended Conductors

Mentally preparing myself, I approached the bus station wondering whether the many foreign students sleeping within the terminal had been there all night. I purchased coffee at a booth where the woman unsuccessfully attempted to get me to add bread to my order. I requested a Coke as a happy compromise, but there seemed to be a miscommunication as she dropped to the ground and began crawling around on the floor desperately emptying the bottom of a large refrigerator. I hastily attempted to perfect my Filipino accent as I tried to make her understand and allow her to recover her morale. I could see the Coke in the middle section of the fridge directly above her.

Pointing in the Philippines is done by protruding the lips in a certain direction. Yes, you read that right—you point with your lips! It is one of the strangest things culturally but it definitely grew on me and I sometimes even do it now much to the amusement of Westerners. I gave up on this occasion and rudely pointed with my hand in an attempt to save the dear lady any further trouble. When she realised what I actually wanted she laughed and apologised. I handed over the grand sum of forty pesos (about fifty pence.) I moved on and purchased a few further items at another stall, I handed the vendor a Christian tract. He immediately stopped serving a customer to read the front of it before thanking me with a smile— Manila is great!

I then faced a dilemma. I could take the slow bus which was perversely marked "express" or the fast bus which hadn't yet arrived. I headed for the ticket desk and saw a long line of people in the queue for Olongapo. Great. Even more of an annoyance were the four members of staff standing behind the glass screen chatting to each other and staring at us in the line, as a lone female cashier scrambled frantically to try and shorten the queue. There were always a lot of customer service people available, but not many who actually wanted to serve customers. Being a foreigner, I generally experienced better customer service than the local people. It might have had something to do with money, but I can't be certain.

I didn't understand why the local people put up with the apathetic customer service and resultant delays as it really could be infuriating. Immigration was the worst—various different lines for slightly different things and if you accidentally got into the wrong line they refused to serve you under any circumstances even if they weren't doing anything else.

Suddenly a booming voice announced that the slow bus was leaving and one by one people were turned away from the desk and ushered towards the waiting bus. I quickly reached the front of the queue and asked for the fast bus *without* insurance. Insurance that cost five pesos (around seven pence) couldn't really be worth much—maybe it would buy me one plaster or a single paracetamol in the event of an emergency. The cashier misunderstood and gave me insurance. I returned the slip politely and asked for my five pesos back. She looked at me as if I had two heads. I realised that her illusions of rich white foreigners had been instantaneously shattered.

During our brief exchange, I was disconcerted to see a white board behind her with the heading "Suspended conductors." The list of names was extensive and each name had a date next to it. It appeared that the conductors were suspended for approximately a week at a time and then allowed to resume their duties. I wondered what their indiscretions were and hoped they had nothing whatsoever to do with road safety.

My bus arrived and I noted a sign in the window "Road testing now." Shouldn't the bus have already been tested as it was already on the road? This and other questions faded away into irrelevance as I boarded the bus, sat down in my numbered seat and was then joined by a VERY large male who proceeded to fall asleep half squashing me in the process. I had to smile though as he frequently leaned into me in a fairly uncomfortable way until I was forced to prod him. Then he occasionally snored waking himself up. At one point, he emitted something like a sneeze cough and then apologised profusely as I tried to hide my smile.

I noticed that the TV at the front was flickering annoyingly with the picture jumping around. It didn't seem to bother the locals most of whom were glued to the screen. I was grateful that it was a harmless, if slightly irritating, Filipino daytime TV show, rather than the violent and gruesome movies that were sometimes shown regardless of the age of the audience. On these occasions, I spent most of the time trying to hide behind my seat so that I didn't inadvertently catch a glimpse of the horror. There was no real discernment in movie and TV viewing even amongst Christians.

The air conditioning was, as usual, turned up far too high and blasting out of vents that were often broken and therefore couldn't be closed. Most regular travellers were wearing extra layers. It tended to be the same in Filipino cinemas. I was relieved to have been allocated a seat as some late comers ended up crouching or standing in the aisle for the entire three-hour journey. I tried it once, it wasn't fun.

At the half way rest-stop, everyone rushed out of the bus to buy snacks as the street vendors clambered in to try and sell snacks to the few that had remained in situ. They enthusiastically cried "mani mani mani" (peanut) thrusting their full buckets of nuts into the passenger's passive faces in the hope of a sale. Other possibilities included boiled eggs, but sometimes Westerners got a bit of a shock when instead of what they were expecting, they discovered a partially grown chicken embryo which had been cooked in its shell. A Filipino delicacy called "balut." As the passengers returned from their rest break, I glanced sideways as a man sat back down next to me and casually observed that he didn't look much like the person that was there before. All became clear as the other man returned and demanded his original seat.

Unfortunately, we were then subjected to a popular form of travelling evangelism with what some might call a "captive audience." Local church denominations employed people to jump aboard the public buses and silently hand every passenger an envelope for donations, or to drop it onto them if they were asleep or refused to take it. Then they used a loud speaker to preach for sometimes up to ten minutes. It was fairly torturous especially when taking a long journey, because different representatives from the same denomination would jump on at every stop along the route and preach the same message. After hearing the message for the third or fourth time there was usually a collective groan amongst the passengers when the next person wearing the badge appeared.

I don't like to unduly criticise any evangelistic practice but I'm not sure that begging from non-Christians going about their daily business is the way to go, especially as many of them felt compelled to give due to their Catholic roots—people with no assurance were sadly often trying to tip God's divine scales in their favour for the afterlife. Removing the burden of good works through various Bible passages was one of the great freedoms that could be offered to Catholics in the Philippines.

Sermon over, I observed that the traffic was totally crazy, my bus sometimes jumped across four lanes to pick up extra passengers, always choosing the very last minute to lurch and nearly colliding with every other vehicle in the process. The solution, a cacophony of extremely loud horns indicating that the owners were about to do something very dangerous and potentially life threatening. The big question that no one seemed to know the answer to was, what was it that each driver was about to do!?

In a near-by lane, twenty-four people were squashed into the back of a small pickup truck. They were packed in like sardines all facing the front with their knees bent awkwardly in front of them. Then there were about a hundred people in a line running parallel to the main road obviously queuing for something. Think of that number of people patiently waiting along the side of the M1 nowhere near a junction and you have the strange image.

A sign at a road block and toll booth proclaimed "Philippine/Japan co-operation project." A Japanese flag fluttered in the breeze causing me briefly to wonder whether I had inadvertently caught the wrong bus and was now at a border crossing. But, wait, the Philippines are islands so that couldn't be right. Geography…hmmm.

Arriving several hours later in Olongapo, I went about my business visiting the youth centre and the street children. Then, I spent a while mentally preparing myself for the long and treacherous bus journey back to Cubao. Travelling in the Philippines is *not* "more fun!"

CHAPTER FIFTEEN

Drop-In Dilemma

Part of my attempted spiritual and cultural integration in Cubao involved volunteering at my church's drop-in ministry on a Thursday evening. A large group, sometimes over one hundred, of the local homeless people came to the church for showers, food and to hear a Bible message. They gathered in a partially enclosed area outside the main church building. Some also attended a Bible study at the church on Monday evenings.

Most of the attendees arrived early so there was time for mingling. They usually collected their small allocated portion of soap and headed for the shower block first. It was difficult to keep order in the cubicles due to the necessity for privacy. Unfortunately, some chose to take drugs or sneak alcohol in with them. There were also a number of men dressed as women with long hair, makeup and high heels. At one of the anniversary celebrations, I recall the senior pastor smiling wryly as he took photos of the group and, indicating the cross dressers, commented "Well what can we do." I'm not aware of any disputes in relation to which gender shower facilities they used, although I'm sure it's not far off.

After showering, the attendees made their way towards the long tables and sat down to chat with their friends. There were also board games like chess and draughts which some enjoyed. The children caused havoc, running wildly around the tables chasing balls or shoes or whatever else they could find to throw. Often, I joined in, swinging the children around until I was dizzy and had to stop, or allowing them to climb up my body until I thought my back might break if I bent any further. I usually ended up being mobbed by the younger ones and unable to move as they hung from every one of my limbs as I begged for mercy.

One small child kept rushing past me, whilst I was sitting talking to some adults, and thumping me hard in the back. I laughed it off for a while but then decided that he shouldn't be allowed to get away with such aggression. I waited for him to make his approach then jumped up to confront him. He ran off, so I chased and captured him intending to turn him upside down or something as I often did when playing with the kids. But, he screamed as if I was murdering him and became hysterical. I put him down immediately, let go and backed away as if he were a bomb. There was a deathly silence throughout the community as I looked around and saw that everyone had stopped what they were doing and all eyes were now on me. His mother came rushing over and offered the unnecessary observation "He doesn't like that." I hastily protested my innocence but resolved not to do *that* again. There was always one who ruined it for everyone, but I did pause and wonder what past experiences had made him react as if he was being killed rather than being given a small taste of his own medicine. He was probably too young to understand that you shouldn't dish it out if you can't take it!

Returning to the adults, I tried to get to know individuals especially women that came alone. Emma was a Catholic and after a good chat one evening, I wanted to give her a Bible, but found that she wouldn't be able to read it due to poor eyesight. We arranged to go to the eye hospital together which resulted in an outpouring of emotion as she had thought that she would go blind, just as her mother had done. She had also believed that nobody cared about her.

Another man was desperate for work having lost his job as a driver. It was virtually impossible to find work once you hit forty, the jobs were mainly given to the younger people. I often saw sign boards advertising shop jobs for those with college degrees! This man still had a valid driving licence but needed a medical check-up and certificate to return to work. After the small amount of money involved was supplied, one of the church deacons accompanied him for the check-up. He appeared a week or so later very excited about having returned to work. But a few months after that he had quit his job and was asking us to help him again because he wanted to seek work abroad. We declined, suggesting instead that he returned to his employer and begged for his job back!

Romey, twenty-two, began attending the drop-in after I met him on the street near the church and invited him. He claimed to be living on the street due to family problems. After his initial reluctance, he started enthusiastically attending every meeting. He was given a Bible and was avidly reading it. I approached the church leaders about helping him to get a job assuming he wanted to work. He agreed to the work that was offered him. He was given two hundred pesos (about three pounds) to buy products to begin selling. He disappeared.

After a few weeks, I was concerned and asked a friend of his where he was. I thought something terrible *must* have happened to him as he had been so keen about attending church and studying the Bible. But apparently, he was fine and had just relocated to another part of town, probably to stop me badgering him. He didn't want to work because he said he needed to sleep. Later, he moved back to the church area looking as dirty and miserable as before. I attempted to re-establish contact but he just responded with grunts. Surprisingly, I didn't feel impatient when I saw him just sad. He looked so hopeless and alone curled up in a ball sleeping outside a shop. His initial response reminded me a lot of the *Parable of the Sower* and the seed that had no depth. It sprang up joyfully at first but the reality of the Christian life was too much like hard work.

I was aware that my church had tried various livelihood programmes. All of the ideas had ultimately ended in failure due to a lack of market for the products and other issues arising from using homeless people to do the work. It was a problem we saw a lot when working with the homeless. They weren't used to steady jobs and didn't know anything about routines, discipline or reliability. They often had unrealistic goals for themselves thinking the "grass was always greener" and many of them didn't even want to work. They were mostly unsaved and therefore didn't have a Biblical reason to work either. The rates of pay were menial and some of the people seemed perfectly happy sleeping on the street and begging for their food.

Many of the attendees had been attending the drop-in since its commencement eleven years before. They announced this proudly to all and sundry. But my first thought on hearing this was; "What has changed in your life since you began attending?" They were hearing the Word of God faithfully preached every week but many of the people were in exactly the same position they were in eleven years before. A lot of them seemed happy and comfortable with their street lives and lack of employment and didn't see the need or hadn't the motivation for change.

Our visitors to the drop-in often came looking for a chat and company rather than anything else, although there were some serial drop-in seekers who went from church to church on a daily basis taking advantage of all of the freebies in the area. I suppose we couldn't blame them as the churches weren't working together. Maybe if I was homeless and hungry, I would do the same thing. A couple of drop-in attendees had eventually become church members but they were few and far between. As previously mentioned, work was definitely needed to try and integrate more of the homeless people into the church.

The dilemma really was how much we as Christians should do for such people and how much we should expect them to do for themselves. Providing additional resources sometimes led to an entitlement attitude and complaints about the levels of service or rejection of the food that was offered and requests for something different. We also needed to identify those who really wanted to change and were prepared to go the extra mile from those who just told us what we wanted to hear. Ultimately, real and lasting change could only come from God if He opened their eyes to the truth.

CHAPTER SIXTEEN

Monday Mayhem

Those from the drop-in who were either more serious about hearing God's Word or who enjoyed company and a free snack on a Monday evening as well as on Thursdays, attended our homeless Bible study. When I first attended the studies, I couldn't quite believe what I was seeing, being used to the very civilised and orderly English style of study. The motley crew of between twenty and forty people, mostly men, traipsed in with varying degrees of punctuality. They often appeared with their worldly belongings in tow so that they didn't get stolen if they left them on the street. Some dragged plastic recyclables that they had collected from the garbage, ready to sell on later or pushed wooden carts containing family members. Many of those doing the heavy work looked to be in their nineties but were really probably just in their sixties or seventies—the hard work had taken its toll on their collective appearance.

There were no care homes for the elderly and obviously no National Health Service. If the older people didn't have family they roamed the streets begging for money, ignored and marginalised by many local people. In a culture where respect for the elderly was high on the agenda and senior citizen's badges earned a twenty percent discount, it seemed contradictory that there was no longer term help.

Amongst the attendees was a man named Jimmy who genuinely (and wrongly) believed himself to be a modern-day apostle. He regularly wore a T-shirt and carried literature proclaiming his status as he espoused his erroneous belief. I was horrified when I first heard and saw what was happening. I raised the issue with the leaders at the study. They listened carefully but didn't seem unduly concerned and didn't really know what to do about it as they had apparently already spoken to him with no resultant change in his behaviour. I had thought he might lead others astray. However, I quickly noticed that whenever the subject arose, usually because he began talking about it, he was mocked and received short shrift from the other homeless people. They were obviously not going to be taken in by this particular false prophet.

I decided to supply personal Bibles to anyone who attended the study for five consecutive weeks. I had a large batch of Tagalog Bibles and it seemed like a perfect opportunity to distribute them. However, after only a month the Bibles that were still visible looked a bit like the people; dirty, tired and had seen better days. But, there was an enthusiasm and quiet joy amongst a few of the attendees, one man had added colourful labels to his Bible so he could find the books easily. He proudly showed me his handiwork. Others had written their names on the spine and had heavily underlined many passages. Some of the Bibles had been well read whilst others were just dragged out for the study. One old man repeatedly tried to claim a second Bible stating that he hadn't been given one. I couldn't ascertain if he had genuinely forgotten or whether he was chancing his arm. Some had no doubt been lost or sold but it was always a risk worth taking for the few that really needed them.

On arrival at the study, the men usually headed straight for the shower block which could only be a good thing judging by the collective smell. Then they sat around a large square table and a man from the church led the study. During the study itself, which lasted for an hour, there was always a lot of disruption. People came and went from the shower block suddenly deciding to have their shower in the middle of the study. A man walked around with an attendance register talking to people as he did so. A church member approached the group and asked a few of the men to go with him to do something. People in the second row slept with T-shirts and towels over their heads, others tried not to fall asleep as they looked on with bleary eyes. The older men squinted in concentration as they persevered in seeking the right page of the Bible when the study was already well underway. Then they found something more interesting and read that instead before commenting enthusiastically to their neighbour about it. A man produced a bright purple comb and began combing his hair which prompted others to copy him. A woman began massaging her partner's arms as he loudly complained of pain. Another old man repeatedly attempted to catch my eye and grinned at me as I looked around. Many people were talking to each other. A few members of the team prepared a snack for afterwards and the whole place became a health hazard as it filled up with smoke from the grill fire. This was the adults, but there were also children and animals present.

A cat appeared and stalked round the table sounding remarkably like a small child and yowling loudly over and over again. It scrabbled noisily around in the garbage that had been neatly stacked against a post awaiting disposal. A rival cat approached and sat at a distance. They began hissing and emitting low growls at each other.

A line of small children traipsed in after a woman who I assumed was the mother of at least one of them. But, she paid little attention to them and treated me as if I was providing a crèche service. This would have been fine but there was nowhere to hold such an activity, so the crèche took place on the fringes of the Bible study. The children spent considerable periods of time lining up their chairs, swapping chairs, trying to get their personal chair as close to mine as was physically possible and doing everything else that you can possibly think of with the chairs that would make as much noise as they were capable of making. Once the chairs were lined up and in the perfect positions with the children seated on them and quiet, I had just a few seconds before one or other of them would get up and leave quickly followed by the others. I don't know where they went, but it wasn't long before they would return and we would go through the entire process again. Then they needed drinks or were hungry or wanted to read aloud. The list of things that children of a little over toddler age can need is extensive.

One small boy with a tiny tuft of hair in the middle of his head, frequently escaped my clutches. He climbed onto a very long table that ran down one side of our meeting place and then ran screaming with delight all the way to the end. If I tried to grab him he manoeuvred quickly out of my reach or burst into tears. Older and no doubt wiser people looking on told me just to let him get on with it as trying to stop him just made more racquet. These children had been given no boundaries and were therefore out of control. Sometimes, I gave up and took to removing them completely and playing hopscotch and other games with them in the street outside.

Yet despite all of the craziness, the study went on. Some of the adults listened attentively and took copious notes. I wondered at the patience of the study leader who never allowed himself to get distracted by any of the things going on around him. Actually, if he had, the study would never have ended. Those that really wanted to listen managed to do so which was the important thing, it was just a complete contrast to Western ways.

During the snacking phase, after the study, I noticed a man eyeing up my old sports bag. He picked it up, examined it and compared it to his own before approaching to tell me that it was a "good bag." I waited for the request that I knew must be in the process of forming in his mind. Sure enough, his bag was "almost broken" and he needed a new one. He asked me if I had any others that I didn't need. I looked closely at his bag which was well worn and very full, bursting at the seams, but it still had a bit of life left in it and there were no holes. I promised to buy him a new one if his broke which seemed to make him happy. I hoped he wouldn't quicken its demise as a result of my promise.

Another woman wrote me a short letter asking if I could fix the wheel on her wooden cart so she could go back to work and provide for her family. I was humbled on learning the cost which was a little over five hundred pesos (just under ten pounds.)

I was surprised by the small things the people asked me for. Their lives were simple and uncomplicated, they didn't want lots of material things but just the basics they needed to survive. I realised a while ago that the more things I had the more cluttered my life was and the more stressed I felt as I had to think about them. Life is about relationships with people, not about things and although much of the time it was not of their own making, the poorer people had an advantage over Westerners in this respect.

CHAPTER SEVENTEEN

Seventeen Jackets Please

I was returning home one day in the pouring rain. As I passed the church, I could see that there was a large group of people beginning to congregate outside the tall metal entrance gates. This didn't surprise me as it was a Monday and the people tended to turn up hours early for the 6pm Bible study having nothing else to do. Usually they just dumped their belongings in a heap and fell asleep on top of each other sprawled across the surrounding pavements waiting for the locked doors to be opened. But on this day, it was raining heavily and there had been a typhoon warning. Normally, my church responded during the calm after the storm by driving around the local area with a soup van, offering a small bit of nourishment and warmth to those less fortunate.

Seeing the people, I was tempted to continue on my way as it was still just 230pm. But, I hesitated for that split second too long and was seen by several of the gang. Then came the inevitable shouts of delight, "ate Natalie, ate Natalie…" (sister.) Having lost my opportunity to disappear, I headed over to the enthusiastic band who I was pleased to see were faithfully carrying their Bibles which were receiving an inevitable soaking. I joined them in gazing at a hastily written sign that had been affixed to the outside of the gate, "Study cancelled, due to typhoon." I had assumed the study would be going ahead as usual as the meeting was held in an area that was out of the elements, but sadly it seemed I was mistaken. Not wanting to disappoint the growing numbers of people, I told them I would double check and quickly phoned the study leader. He confirmed that it was cancelled. I related the fact that the people were already there and that some of them had travelled a long way, thinking he would relent. But, it was not to be.

I looked at the miserable bunch in front of me, as they now huddled in several groups, wet, cold and shivering due to mostly being clad only in T-shirts and thin layers. I delivered the bad news about the study but felt terrible as I saw their hopelessness. Thinking there was nothing I could do, I was about to turn away and leave the scene. However, I then saw an older lady shivering in her ragged, thin, T-shirt and hugging herself in an effort to keep warm.

Allowing an ounce of compassion to seep out, but only an ounce as with the numbers of people surrounding me I didn't know where more than that might lead. I asked the woman whether she had other clothing and how she was planning to find her way back to wherever she was sleeping. She, of course, didn't have other layers but she resisted the urge to respond that had she had them she would have been wearing them. I was grateful that she didn't choose to highlight the absurdity of my question.

With a sigh, knowing where all of this was heading, I invited her to accompany me so that I could buy her a jacket or jumper from the nearby Ukay Ukay (second hand clothes.) My poor communication skills due to my limited vocabulary, meant that I hadn't been able to keep my suggestion at a level that only she could hear. In any event, the other people were by now watching me intently, wondering what I was planning to do to help them. Taking advantage of the situation, several of the adult men then surrounded me with exaggerated shivering, as they hugged themselves in the same way that the lady had been doing. They complained that they were also cold. I resisted the impulse to tell them to "man up" and that they didn't need to make spectacles of themselves in order for me to help them. After a half-hearted attempt to point out to the men that the lady was in greater need due to her age and threadbare clothing, I mentally calculated the financial cost before succumbing. I knew I would have to buy clothing for all of them. They had by this point started chanting "we want jackets" or the Filipino equivalent which turned into loud cheers as I announced that there would be coats all round!

I felt a bit embarrassed as I led the untidy, drenched and by now very excited group along the pavement, especially when I ran into two of my housemates who looked bemused. By the time we arrived at the store, there were seventeen people in the gang, as others had mysteriously appeared as if by magic, at the mention of a freebee. On arrival, I informed the store manager, (who fortunately I already knew,) that each person was allowed to choose one jacket or jumper. I politely requested that she count them out as they left and assured her that I would pay the bill at the end. She smiled but swiftly moved to guard the door to make sure that what had been agreed was what actually happened, I didn't blame her.

Then I turned and addressed the motley crew who were patiently waiting at the entrance to the store. In a loud voice so they couldn't claim later not to have heard me, I made them promise that they wouldn't sell the items afterwards knowing full well that some of them would anyway. The possibility always had to be factored into a decision to help, but most of the time it was worth helping anyway for the sake of the genuine. After making the promise, the crowd of mostly men swarmed into the shop. They spent a while browsing before most of them selected very large coats that were obviously too big, but would hopefully keep them warm.

As they left the store sporting their new bulky outerwear, some of which were bright red in colour, each said thankyou. I encouraged them to view the gifts as a blessing from God. There was only one man left who couldn't find anything to his liking, probably because the quicker guys had cleared an entire rack of coats. So, I went through the other racks with him only to hear him say "parang babae" (it looks like a girls) around fifty times. I told him "parang lalaki" (I think you can guess that one) but he didn't believe me and turned his nose up at everything. I was tempted to leave him in his thin T-shirt, but as he was an older man I took him to a nearby new clothes shop. I eventually managed to get him a long-sleeved T-shirt for just slightly more than I had paid for the other items of clothing. I kept half an eye on the door, anticipating a selection of the others to come rushing in after us to swap, complain or demand the extra money. But nobody did which was nice. They were all very grateful and made me pose for a photo with them wearing their "new jackets." The total cost was just a little over twenty pounds (around fifteen hundred pesos.) It was a definite bargain!

I found the lady that had unintentionally triggered the clothing run, to check that she was now sufficiently warm. However, she immediately and brazenly asked if I could buy her a coffee. Surprised by her boldness, I asked how much it was before the quick mental calculation for seventeen plus coffees. I nodded my assent as I could feel that despite the jumper, her hands were still freezing cold. I again led the throng to a street coffee machine which looked like it had seen better days but offered coffee for just five pesos. It crossed my mind that most people, even in the Philippines, could afford to buy a decent cup of coffee from somewhere other than an old disused machine. Vending was a slow process as I stood by the machine inserting the coins in the rain. The people took their time to choose their coffee or hot chocolate, probably due to the novelty value as someone else was buying it for them. They then took shelter under a nearby roof waiting for their friends. Concluding the long line, I grabbed my chocolate and finally made good my escape noting that the total cost for all eighteen coffees had been around one pound.

After this day, I was constantly asked for clothes, shown holes in clothes or defects in bags and received requests for hot drinks. I refused as I didn't want to start a trend. My church had already been catering adequately for these people for many years and I didn't want to draw attention away from the good work that was being done.

It was a lesson again about the need to draw boundaries and to be involved in partnering with people who are involved in long term ministry. It is easy to make grand gestures and throw money or material resources into situations but sometimes this disrupts the long-term work and can negatively impact those who are already investing in the people. We need to be wise in our use of God's resources for His glory.

CHAPTER EIGHTEEN

The 29kg Girl

Somehow, the people in the sorriest circumstances always seemed to live practically on my doorstep in Cubao. They inhabited the surrounding alleys and streets, or at least this is how it appeared. Maybe it was just that there were so many needs. One day, I saw a large group of homeless people gathered at a petrol station a few minutes' walk from my house. The extremely dirty and malnourished small children approached, grabbing my arms and asking for money and food. Making small talk, I looked around and sized up the situation. I returned regularly to the area, trying to connect the people with the Thursday drop-in. Some of them came sporadically.

During one visit, I had spotted Dina, a nineteen-year-old, single mum, in the middle of the group. I had initially been shocked by her appearance—she looked like a child due to her emaciated state. She had permanent dark circles under her eyes, and we discovered later at the clinic, that she weighed just twenty-nine kilograms. I suspected that she must have severe anorexia or advanced TB and found it difficult to even look at her. The others said that she hadn't been able to stop coughing for around a month, but they didn't seem unduly concerned. There was a sense in which people had become desensitised to these situations as they were all around them on a daily basis.

I bought Dina food and medicine extracting a solemn promise from the others not to share the items. She coughed all the way to the doctor's appointment and had to keep stopping every few steps to do so. I feared it might be too late for her to get medical attention and wondered whether we would even make it to the clinic. When we finally arrived, I explained that Dina needed a check-up and outlined her symptoms at which point the staff asked me what I wanted them to do. I found this a little strange as I had little medical knowledge and would have guessed that their judgement would be better than mine. I asked them to do whatever they needed to try and diagnose the problem.

Later I was called in to join Dina in a consultation. They staff had thought she was a child due to her size and the paediatric doctor wanted to know how I was connected to her. I explained that I was a missionary and wanted to help. The doctor seemed more interested in learning about my missionary work and England than his patient. But I knew I needed to bear with him and that he would eventually tend to the important matter. The fascination with me over, Dina had some tests and an X-ray.

The next day I returned to the clinic alone to collect the results and was met with grave faces all around. Dina's condition was serious and she needed to be taken to the hospital straight away as an in-patient. The X-ray showed a large black abnormality down one side of her lung. I went quickly to find Dina and show her the X-ray. On breaking the news to Dina and the other women (including her mother,) none seemed particularly concerned. It was even difficult to persuade one of them to accompany her to the hospital. I spent a while ensuring that they really understood how serious the situation was and that they were actually going to attend the hospital. I was frustratingly unable to accompany them due to a prior commitment. I left enough money for the trip and prescription and prayed that they would go.

Reflecting, I realised that I was always going to struggle with the apparent lack of concern of some Filipino's about the circumstances of their relatives and friends. I wondered if they had become hardened by the various calamities they had had to face over the years. I knew that serious illness and death was sadly a regular feature in the lives of many Filipinos. Even more so in the lives of those that lived and worked on the street, but it was hard at times not to judge this indifference and lack of empathy. I suppose that feeling emotional about a situation doesn't necessarily achieve anything, but the blank looks I received when detailing something which to me was really shocking could be difficult to cope with at times.

Dina had asked me to rent a place for her family but I just couldn't do it. It wouldn't have been possible to supervise them effectively and she had numerous relatives that would have ended up being included in the arrangements. I would have attempted it if it was just Dina and her baby, but I also hadn't been able to confirm whether or not the Dina and her family was linked to a large group of solvents users in the area. Walking amongst a pile of their bodies one day, I had been appalled to see not only boys and girls abusing the drugs but adults in the midst. It was a different ball game to Olongapo, here there was no attempt to hide the bags of solvents on site of a foreigner. I was even offered drugs by some of the more brazen youths. Working men in the vicinity called greetings to me as I moved amongst the wretched individuals in various states of comatose. It was as if it was the most natural thing in the world to be taking place on a street corner. What a sorry mess.

After the day I delivered Dina's clinic results, every time I saw her I was relieved that she was still alive but also so disappointed to see no visible improvement. She had been to the church once but hadn't come back due to being simply too exhausted, I could see why as she was like a bag of skin and bones. I didn't know how she even had energy to move at all. I settled for encouraging her to ask God directly for help and continued praying for her.

CHAPTER NINETEEN

Death Comes to Cubao

Although Dina and others who seemed always to be living on the edge of death, survived, albeit with a poor quality of life. Others were taken in unpredictable fashion and often at younger ages than we would expect in the West. Living in the Philippines made me grateful for the NHS with all its faults and failings. In England, I never had to worry that I might lose my house or livelihood if I became seriously ill or that I might be refused treatment on the basis that I wouldn't be able to pay for it. Our medical care is also comparatively advanced resulting in much lower mortality rates. For example, a twelve-year-old girl living in one of my church's homes near Manila, died from a thyroid storm during the early stages of an investigation into her symptoms.

Emergency insurance is available in the Philippines but most of the poorer communities are not covered. Hospital bills are ridiculously expensive and patients held until the bill is paid. Churches often hold collections for members facing medical expenses. I was always staggered by the figures involved—a pastor whose son fell off a roof injuring his head was left with a bill of two hundred thousand pesos (three thousand pounds,) after a short hospital stay.

Unfortunately, just as in the West, there are also unscrupulous doctors or alleged miracle workers who take advantage of people. One recently married lady with breast cancer was offered expensive guaranteed treatment despite the illness having advanced. She and her husband desperately appealed for funds and although some money was raised, the lady died. These heartless individuals preyed on people's vulnerabilities telling Christians that it was because they didn't have enough faith that they remained sick or their loved one had died. There was no proper regulation and the bereaved parties tended to be grateful to the fraudsters for having offered them hope even though it had been short-lived.

The range of illnesses is broader, diseases that have been virtually eradicated in Western nations rear their ugly heads from time to time in the Philippines—rabies and tuberculosis to name just a couple. Then there are diseases due to the climate and presence of mosquitoes—dengue fever and malaria being amongst the most feared. Despite a widespread belief that you can only catch dengue once, it actually gets more serious the more times you have it and there are a lot of different strains. A person could catch all of the strains in their lifetime—people ended up hoping and praying for the less deadly ones. A Bible student at my church caught dengue for the second time. His platelet count went down to just twelve thousand when the average person has between one hundred and fifty thousand and three hundred and fifty thousand. He made a full recovery but lives in fear of catching it again as there is no vaccine.

A seven-year-old street child who had been attending our drop-in ministry for a number of years, was in hospital for eight days being pumped full of fluids. She had become malnourished over a period of time due to neglect by her family. Church volunteers signed up for twenty-four-seven hospital guard duties. It is almost mandatory in the Philippines for someone to accompany the sick person at all times, apparently to prevent interference by any third party or theft of their belongings. The child eventually died despite our fervent prayers, we had reached her too late and nothing could be done to prevent the decline in her health.

Sadly, the tragedy of the little girl's death was then turned into a political debacle as the government refused to pick up the tab for the cost of her burial. It was around eight days before Christian Compassion Ministries decided to take responsibility and obtain permission for her body to be released from the morgue. Even if her family members had been interested, they couldn't afford to deal with the practicalities. In the end, one of the social workers persuaded his boss to allow CCM to take over as he was so distressed by the handling of the case and wanted to give her an element of dignity. It was truly appalling for organisations to be arguing over the cost of burying a dead child.

I was asked to accompany the social worker to the burial as a representative of the church. We first went in search of family members to give them one last chance to take part in the procedures. We eventually located the girl's mother, but giving some ridiculously trivial reason in the circumstances, she refused to accompany us. The whole day was surreal. The tiny open casket which I refused to look directly into, didn't look big enough to hold a real person. I just caught a glimpse of a tumble of hair at one end of the box and couldn't bear to see anymore. The partial image had reminded me of a rag doll rather than a dead child, but I, perhaps selfishly, turned my head away terrified of a permanent imprint on my mind.

The cemetery was unusual, well at least to a Western mindset. The people were not buried in the ground. The coffins were stacked five or six persons high on shelves, in a style that reminded me more of a mortuary than anything else. The caskets were inserted into a slot in a wall with hundreds of others. The grave was then marked with a stone and sometimes writing was added. The walls ran in parallel lines that were spaced close together a bit like being in a supermarket. The walls ran as far as the eye could see and towered far above the heads of any visitors.

The little girl's funeral consisted of a few church members standing around singing hymns and praying for her absent family. We went through the motions, but I think I was probably in shock as I felt numb throughout the proceedings. I just wished that things could've been different and sought desperately to remember the little lively girl from the drop-in, rather than the lifeless form that had now been deposited into a wall forever. The attitude of her family made me realise that there would be no visitors after we departed. When a child dies in England, they are usually gone but not forgotten. In this case I couldn't be sure, but I had hope that she had heard the Gospel and that at least she would be remembered by the faithful staff at the drop-in.

The younger ones were of course more tragic and unexpected, but there were also sudden deaths of adults that left great holes in people's lives. Emily, a grandmother who had been one of the first street people to become a member at my church, died in her sleep one night. She was probably in her fifties and had been caring for numerous grandchildren. A familiar face around the church and a visible representative of the "former homeless" community. Suddenly, all the talk was about what to do with the children and whether or not they should be taken into state care. Prior to that there were the very long-winded funeral arrangements.

Filipino funerals usually last seven days or more. Every day mourners attend the house of the deceased to offer condolences to the family. The families are expected to host and feed their numerous guests. They often end up appealing to the church to cover the cost of satisfying the needs of the many well-wishers. In this case, the open casket remained visible in the house throughout and people formed orderly queues to line up and peer into it. When my turn came, I declined to view the body of Emily preferring to remember her as she had been. A fellow mourner, on seeing my reluctance, commented "Oh, don't worry, she's been made up and looks really beautiful." I stuck to my guns, even during my policing days, I had never been that comfortable around dead bodies.

At every funeral, Christian pastors took the evangelistic opportunity to preach every day of the seven. The result was that every time there was a death in the local community, the church that had had the most involvement with any members of the family was rushing round trying to organise preachers for the next seven days. This often meant cancelling other church functions or juggling responsibilities and there was no time for preparation. I wondered whether it might be more effective to restrict the preaching to a single evening. Due to the religion traditions in the country, people didn't seem to be listening as it was more of a formality. I had to remind myself that it is the Holy Spirit that convicts, and God that draws people to Himself and that as long as the Word is being preached, He is at work.

Death is a visible reality in the Philippines and people are not afraid to talk or even to joke about it. Placing an open casket in the midst of people whilst preaching about heaven and hell, certainly reminded them of their own mortality in a way that nothing else could have done. I wondered whether the practice would open some closed hearts if it were adopted in the UK, but realised that our English sensibilities wouldn't tolerate it.

CHAPTER TWENTY

What's That Smell?

In late 2014, after I had been living in Manila for around six months, we were approaching Christmas. I had been planning a big trip to visit some of the "rugby boys" still in rehab and others who had unfortunately been released but ended up back there a few months later. My charity had raised funds for a special day to visit them with some of their family members and to give gifts. We were also going to start a Christian library.

The planning for this event involved going back and forth to the local shops carrying large bags and boxes of items for storage at my house pending the big day. I didn't really want to be distracted by anything else as I had a lot to organise. A team from my new church were planning to accompany me for the first time and it was going to be a great opportunity to introduce them to the ministry with the "rugby boys."

However, I couldn't ignore two ragged and dirty figures with a baby that had inconveniently appeared at the end of my road in recent weeks. I saw them every time I passed by with my loaded bags of material items. I didn't feel bad about the things I was carrying knowing they were for a good cause, but the contrast was striking. These people clearly had nothing and had been reduced to begging for their daily food. I had everything and the ability to buy more if I wanted.

I stopped to talk to them establishing that they were all from one family that had fallen on hard times. Mary, twenty-one, said that their house had been burnt to the ground forcing them onto the street. Her husband had left her. Her companions were her eighteen-year-old brother and her one year old baby. There was really no way for me to verify their story and I didn't really need to, they were obviously in need. Having got close enough to talk to them, I could see that the baby was very dirty and had the start of a severe scalp infection. At first, I just bought them some food and medicine and invited them to my church which was just a hundred metres away from their chosen sleeping spot.

On the Sunday, I came out of the church service and was immediately surrounded by a crowd of street children desperately trying to tell me something. I was still trying to piece together their bits of English using my pitiful understanding of Tagalog when the mystery was solved. The children led me to the family at the end of the street. Apparently, they had attended the church but had arrived late and therefore hadn't been able to gain access.

I asked Mary how she was doing which seemed a stupid question and felt totally inadequate. It was like asking someone how they are feeling when someone close to them has just died. Fortunately for me, Filipino's don't say things like "Well how do you think I'm doing? My house burnt down, I have no food, no money, and no work, my husband left me, my baby is sick, I'm living on a dirty street corner reduced to begging and a typhoon is coming."

The temptation to offer them lodgings for a while was very great especially with the Christmas period approaching. But, there were similar situations everywhere and I had to try and use my head not just my heart. I also needed to think about my housemates who had already graciously tolerated the constant arrival of various street children that showed up by invitation or more often without one. I decided to take them in for Christmas if the storm worsened and that I would definitely invite them to our place for Christmas day regardless.

They attended the church on the following Sunday. I was delighted to see them but as I looked at their dirty ragged clothes, I despaired. I could see that no amount of cleaning would get them ready for the service. I knew that some in the congregation would not take kindly to being forced to endure the smell of weeks on the street as I had discovered on a previous occasion. I had been sitting next to a small boy that had been very excited about attending church.

Jack, thirteen, like most Filipino children, was from a Catholic background. He had been using solvents on occasion before I met him. He had appeared during the previous week with his strange gait recognisable even from a distance. He was wearing his holey, dirty clothes with terrible grazing all over his face. He said he had collided with a tricycle (motorised with side cart,) or more likely the driver had crashed into him. Over time, the street kids tended to become invisible to motorists, not worth the trouble it took *not* to run them over.

He had come running up to me with his usual big smile and enthusiastic greeting and asked expectantly and with a level of urgency "Ate (sister) Natalie, can I please come to the church service with you on Sunday because of my sin." Although I knew that his statement was probably due to thinking church was a place for confession, I reflected that our world would be a very different place if everyone recognised their sin as a reason for going to church!

On arriving at church, Jack had had a shower but had obviously not made the best of it. A church member who will remain nameless had turned to the smiling boy seated in the row behind him, and asked him whether he had had a shower. When he answered proudly in the affirmative, the man had turned back around without responding and held his nose through the rest of the service. My heart broke for Jack but I don't think he was old enough to fully understand the slight. Afterwards, I received complaints and determined not to let it happen again. In the man's defence, the smell was gag-inducing and I wondered what Jack had actually used to attempt to wash himself. It definitely couldn't have been anything even slightly resembling soap!

The sad thing was that in contrast to the other children, Jack actually wanted to be there. He sat next to me mostly quietly and listened to my instructions. He tried to sing the songs and looked at the words in the Bible, a tough task as it was in English. He at least attempted to listen to the sermon. He fell asleep at intervals but at least he tried to stop himself by sharply jerking his head backwards and forwards, which made me laugh as he didn't realise that I had seen him. Jack was a grateful boy which was a rarity amongst his peers. When I told him that Jesus loved him and had a plan for him. He looked at me to see if it could really be true. He wanted so much to believe it.

Returning from my quick trip down memory lane, I decided that a brief visit to Ukay Ukay (used clothes shop) was on the cards. At least I was supporting the local economy, but I hoped I wouldn't be judged too harshly for shopping on Sunday. I rushed them to the shop and waited as they gathered some clean(ish) and more suitable attire. Then we rushed back, cringing as the senior pastor walked past us as we headed out of the shop. There was a slight moment of awkwardness as he hastily explained that *he* was going to buy medicine for his wife and I gave what I hoped was an acceptable explanation for my Sunday trading. I was pleased that he smiled at my companions. Afterwards, I realised that I had never seen the senior pastor in the street before, typical.

Back at church, Tracey and Charlotte had also decided to join us with their friends. I wondered how on earth I could supervise all of them and ensure the new guests were made to feel welcome in what would no doubt be a very strange environment for them. We ended up taking up nearly an entire back row and I sat in the middle— street kids on one side and street guest family with a small child on the other. Needless to say, the service was a nightmare for me as I struggled to pay attention and worried about all manner of things. It was after this service that a few of my friends took pity on me and began volunteering to sit separately with one or other of the street children when I had too many to cope with. They really needed one to one attention throughout and as my church didn't allow colouring books or gadgets for the children, I could only give them notebooks and pens which they abused wholeheartedly. Until these moments, I would never have guessed how much disruption could be caused by such simple everyday items.

After the service, I took advantage of the on-hand translation to get a better grip of the circumstances of the family. I had been piecing things together gradually and my biggest shock so far had been establishing that the younger brother was actually a sister! She had her hair cut so short and there had been no attempts made to correct my many mistakes in relation to her gender. It didn't help that there is no specific pronoun for he or she in Tagalog, it is just a generic "siya." That is why Filipinos often use the wrong gender in English or interchange them throughout a sentence, referring to someone as a "he" but later saying "she" or "her".

The discovery actually helped in terms of my Christmas plans as one of my concerns had been hosting the family in an all-girl house. It emerged that the sisters and baby had been living with an aunt, but had run away after an argument. I don't know what happened to the fire story. I think maybe they had been living independently but had been forced to take refuge with the aunt after the fire. They were reluctant to return but I spent a lot of time pointing out the serious potential consequences of remaining on the street especially for the baby who had been recovering well from her scalp infection, due to the medicine. I also took a bit of a risk by suggesting that the aunt would be relieved to hear from them and might welcome them back if they apologised for whatever it was that had caused offense. In saying this, I was aware that due to the culture, some Filipinos would rather estrange themselves forever than go through the shame of an apology.

In the end, we did persuade them to at least attempt to return to the aunt in time for Christmas. I saw them onto a jeepney and paid their fare. Having already supplied them with Gospel literature and ensured they heard about saving hope in Jesus verbally, I prayed for them and wished them well. I had no way of knowing whether they would reach their destination. For all I knew, they might get off the jeepney around the next corner and choose somewhere else to hunker down for the night. Only this time, they would likely choose somewhere where they wouldn't be accosted by a white woman trying to help them, and drag them into church. I didn't see the family again, but the seed had been planted and I prayed that God might cause it to grow at the right time.

CHAPTER TWENTY-ONE

Camp Chaos

I had been planning for some time for Joel and Paul, two of my former "rugby boys" to visit me in Cubao. They were now fifteen and sixteen and had been making good progress in Olongapo. I wanted to acknowledge their achievements—they were regularly attending school and had managed to stay away from the solvents and keep out of trouble. Unfortunately, obstacles kept popping up which delayed our plans. The social worker was worried about the boys travelling alone on a public bus. I found it difficult to take her concern seriously considering that prior to our intervention, they had been living on the street and addicted to drugs. On the other hand, my experiences with Manila's buses forced me to hesitate as I tried to reassure her. The matter was eventually taken out of our hands, at least temporarily, because Paul contracted dengue fever from an infected mosquito bite. He ended up in hospital for several weeks, postponing the visit once again.

Our annual three-day church drop-in camp was fast approaching and I was suddenly inspired to invite the Olongapo boys to join us. Their social worker reluctantly consented seeing as Paul had by now fully recovered from his "near death experience." He had survived the dreaded dengue, and the dangers of travelling on crazy buses must've seemed trivial in comparison.

Therefore, two very excited boys arrived in Cubao ready for camp. I was astonished by the progress Paul had made with his English. It was so much easier to communicate with him—he even acted as translator for Joel. Both boys were very calm and polite. They even offered to clean up the cat mess in the downstairs bathroom so they could have showers—I think my housemates had been trying to train Chiqui to use the bathroom and as it wasn't my bathroom I stayed out of it.

We headed off to camp joining the throng of seventy or so homeless people on the rented bus. The camp was held at a large centre with grounds and a swimming pool. The accommodation was very basic—bunk beds in dormitories—but it was catered so we didn't have to worry about cooking. There were to be topic based Bible studies and other activities each day. The campers had to somehow manage to avoid smoking, drinking and taking other substances for the three-day period. I suspected that some of them found ways around the rules, but unless they were caught in the act there wasn't much that could be done.

Paul and Joel were timid and quiet in comparison to the regular campers. They remained separate from the main group. I was relieved that they had each other for company as I couldn't supervise them constantly. They enjoyed the swimming pool and I was keen to join them as they splashed around. After checking that it wasn't against the rules or against general camp etiquette, I prayed a prayer of protection from disease—not a harsh judgement but a reality. Then I jumped in, becoming the first non-former-homeless volunteer to do so.

This decision caused mass excitement as the younger children swarmed all over me. I tried for the next hour to evade their clutches and to actually do some swimming. Having evaded them temporarily, I raced Paul and Joel across the pool. I knew that they were capable of high speeds having seen them daily in the polluted river back in Olongapo. I confided that I had longed to join them in the water even then, but was prevented from doing so by rules and regulations whilst living on the Logos Hope ship.

After swimming, I saw the two boys sitting alone and went over to chat. They were finding the camp tough going. Paul said that there was "no joy and peace" and that the campers were like a "scrabble." He indicated a desperate grabbing motion with his hands and I realised he meant a "rabble." I thought about the meal lines—every person collecting every meal tried to jostle and push their way to the front with no consideration or concern for anyone else. I realised that the boys were right in this respect, but kept my amusement to myself, that two former "rugby boys" were now such reformed characters that they were piously judging others for being too rowdy. I encouraged them to try and make friends with the people, who were in general pretty harmless, but just used to a different way of life.

On the final evening, we had a "fun talent night." The campers were divided into groups and spent hours preparing to act out a drama for the entertainment of everyone else. Left to their own devices, the performances turned into a spiritual disaster. Some of the Bible teaching at the camp had been about homosexuality and women in leadership roles. The campers were keen to show that they had been listening. In a strangely convoluted form of application that would never have entered my mind, a number of them dressed up as the opposite gender or acted out the part of a female minister. They then demonstrated that this was wrong practice, by committing various sins in these roles. I didn't understand much of what was going on but that was the gist. Paul and Joel looked totally bemused as they hid at the back of the room and thereby avoided being dragged onto the stage and forced to participate.

Before the end of the camp, we discussed the two boys' future plans and the time that they had thus far spent at the Centre for Youth in Olongapo. Both of them were struggling, it was the same issues; little food, little activity and little freedom. At a loss to know what to do to help them, I asked what their ideal solution would be. Paul thoughtfully suggested that it might be possible for the two of them to live with his grandma, if suitable accommodation could be found.

Our serious conversation was disrupted by a male adult camper that I didn't recognise. He had sidled up to me whilst I was talking to the boys. I waited to see what he wanted and when he didn't say anything I asked him, probably a little sharply, if he was okay. Seemingly unaware that he had interrupted us, he asked me some bland personal questions. Paul and Joel looked on, vaguely interested. I answered that I was busy having a discussion with the two boys about something important. Having explained this, I expected him to leave and waited patiently for him to do so. But he remained rooted to the spot, continuing to stare at me. I turned slightly away from the man, thinking that if I ignored him he would become embarrassed and slink away.

I continued trying to talk to the boys but was obviously slightly distracted by the man's presence in our small group. The man then suddenly interjected to ask whether he could kiss me. The boys found the turn of events hilarious and were unable to hide their incredulity at the man's boldness, as well as their sniggers, as I hastily declined the man's ridiculous request. I was becoming seriously irritated and starting to feel harassed, I told the man quite clearly to go away. He hesitated before amending his suggestion— maybe he could cuddle me instead. I think in his mind this was a good compromise as I wasn't willing to kiss him. I wondered at his persistence and then saw that his friends were watching his progress (or lack of it) from a distance. They had all congregated outside their accommodation about fifty metres away and were grinning and signalling to him to continue. Realising that my only option was to continue talking to the boys elsewhere, I made it abundantly clear I wasn't interested in continuing the fruitless discussion and quickly moved away.

Throughout the camp, leaders and volunteers alike communicated how impressed they were with the two boys. Although struggling with the camp they continued to be obedient, doing exactly as they were told and listening carefully to the Christian messages. They stood in stark contrast to many of the other campers, as they were only too fully aware. I was thrilled to witness the changes in both of them—not only had they grown in stature, but in maturity, and it seemed in faith. They were both keen to learn and to make up for lost time. But were they really ready to live independently, and was I willing to take the risk?

The camp finally over and with some serious decisions to make, we piled into the coach to head back to Cubao. I saw further evidence of the "scrabble" Paul had been talking about. A small quantity of snacks and drinks were distributed from the front of the bus, and the campers bickered, argued and even fought physically as they tried to snatch as many as possible for themselves.

The whole camp experience had really been an eye opener for the boys (and for me.) They had seen "street-life in Manila" up close and personal and realised how different it was from living in Olongapo even when they had been on the street. I was in awe of the volunteers who had by now been running the camp for over a decade. I don't think there are many people in the world who would even have attempted putting such a crazy idea into practice.

After the camp in 2015 a woman was stabbed by her ex-partner as we got off the bus in Cubao. I attempted to find the crime scene and secure it—normal procedure in England—but this didn't seem to be a high priority for the Filipinos. Nor was calling the police. They just rushed around arranging for the injured person to go to hospital, worrying about medical bills, and discussing who might be the suspect. The same woman was stabbed several weeks later by the same suspect who had still not been arrested. Then, in 2016, someone sadly died during the camp. By comparison, it seemed 2014 had been a mild year.

CHAPTER TWENTY-TWO

The Big House

After the camp and prior to the two boys returning to Olongapo, they attended my church. At the end of the service, Paul said to me in English, "There will be a judgement day." I stopped abruptly and turning to face him asked, "Do you understand what that means?" He responded confidently "Yes I do." He also asked me what being "born again" meant as although both boys had made professions of faith, I hadn't used the terminology with them. They had obviously heard it during the camp. Paul also told me that he wanted to be baptised!

Having discussed Paul and Joel's future plans during the camp and witnessed their apparent growth in maturity and responsibility. I decided it was time to give them a shot at living independently in Olongapo. They were still minors, as I had been reminded when Joel had passed me a note which read "Please promise that you won't ever go away or leave us." At this stage, I planned to remain in the Philippines long term, but I couldn't make promises in case God called me elsewhere. Still, requests like this obviously tugged at my heart strings making me want to offer him the assurance he was seeking. Independent living would only be possible if I could persuade an adult to join the boys. I couldn't take on the responsibility due to my gender and lack of biological connection to them. The most obvious person seemed to be Paul's grandma who was homeless and sold small items on the street for her daily needs. Naively, I thought we would be killing two birds with one stone by providing accommodation for Grandma as well.

However, there was a slight complication. Paul's father, who had disappeared when Paul was a baby, had recently been seen wandering around in Olongapo. Paul had been left to grow up without either parent—we believe his mother had been working as a prostitute before sadly dying from illness at a relatively young age. On his re-emergence, reports suggested that Paul's father appeared to be ill, he was extremely thin and emaciated, most likely, he was suffering from tuberculosis. Paul sucked his cheeks in to demonstrate how his father had looked when he had seen him. He became very quiet and I could see that he was struggling to talk about how he felt about having seen his father after such a long time. Rather than being angry about the abandonment all those years ago, Paul was apparently quick to forgive and desperate now to help his father and grandma. He was frustrated by his inability to do anything practically to change their sad situations. When we had the discussion, he tried to hide his emotion and blamed it on the spicy chilli he was eating. Seeing Paul's care and concern for his father, I knew that he would need to be included in the living arrangements.

I realised that it was time to meet Paul's relatives and assess the situation prior to making any commitments. Myself and the two boys therefore set off for Olongapo. On the bus, the boys somehow managed to immediately lose one of their tickets just as the conductor was asking to see it. They gave up looking for it straightaway, as if expecting me to just buy another one without a second thought. I'm sure the other passengers were amused when I forced the boys to get out of their seats. I began thoroughly searching everything with a lot of enthusiasm in complete contrast to their half-hearted efforts. I knew the ticket couldn't have just vanished into thin air but they didn't seem to grasp this. I briefly wondered whether renting a house for them was wise if they couldn't even look after a bus ticket, but pushed this to the back of my mind.

After a fruitless search, I was tapped on the shoulder by Paul who, looking sheepish, produced the ticket. I asked him where he had found it and he pointed to where *I* had been sitting as if I was responsible for losing it. I asked him directly whether he had actually found it in his pocket. Ashamed, he nodded. I encouraged him to laugh about it but it is hard in a shame culture to laugh at your own mistakes. I think he saw the funny side when he realised I was no longer annoyed.

We arrived in Olongapo and headed straight for "The Triangle," to look for Grandma. This is an area where a lot of rough sleepers hung around during the day and bedded down at night. I saw a large crowd of people around the woman I recognised as Paul's grandma. Notably, there were also at least two very thin, sickly looking men hanging around the vicinity. Paul greeted them unenthusiastically, I guessed that one of them was likely to be his father.

After the extremely brief introductions, I was unceremoniously asked if I could pay for a prescription for one of the men who turned out to be Paul's uncle. It was suggested that he probably had tuberculosis and one didn't need to be a doctor to see that he was very ill. The other man confirmed that he was Paul's father. In fact, the large group of people made up Paul's entire extended family. I was really surprised by this revelation, as I had been under the impression that Paul didn't really have any living family members. The implication had also been that he wasn't close to the few that had been dubiously linked to him by the social services department.

Paul's grandma helpfully agreed to be the mature, responsible adult that was needed to accompany Paul and Joel, and to look after Paul's father, in our hypothetical living arrangement. I suggested we go and search for a suitable property immediately as it might take some time. I wasn't planning to join the folk in "The Triangle" when they turned in for the night. In reality, my plan was really very ambitious, as I didn't have local identification or even a local address. Most sensible landlords would not be willing to enter into this type of arrangement with a strange white woman. I could disappear at any moment leaving them to foot bills and evict difficult tenants, but we had prayed about it so we went in faith. Slightly annoyingly, we were accompanied by a loud and opinionated friend of Grandma's. Her English was quite good, though, which was extremely useful in the circumstances. I determined to put up with her constant stream of opinions about anything and everything without complaint.

I realised early on that Grandma wasn't going to be able to cope with walking around looking at properties, especially in the heat of the day. Within ten minutes, we had found a one bedroomed property which was very small, cramped and dark. Grandma and the friend started making arrangements to move in, but I wanted to see what else was available. I knew that if the two boys didn't have their own space the living arrangement wouldn't last long. I didn't want them to settle on an unsuitable property just because they didn't want to walk around for a bit longer. We continued our trek, with the friend loudly reminding me about the first property every few paces. Then we were nearly eaten alive by some dogs at another place whilst making enquiries. I eventually sent Grandma and her loud friend back from whence they had come and continued the search alone with Paul and Joel. This proved to be much more peaceful, if not initially successful.

I had discovered when looking for my own house in Cubao that due to being a foreigner it was assumed also that I was rich. I had to hide nearby and send the boys in to make the enquiries. If I didn't appear at the right moment of the conversation, the boys would be laughed at due to their ages and lack of knowledge of house-renting procedures. But, when I did make my presence known, the prices mysteriously doubled or tripled. It was really a catch twenty-two situation without Grandma. Not many landlords wanted to rent to two teenage boys, especially boys that they might have previously seen in the area on the street taking solvents!

After viewing a few places, we had a better idea of local prices. Eventually, we settled on a really nice two up two down place within a private compound. There were several houses inside the gated entrance and the landlady lived in one of the others. The two large dogs in a cage just inside the entryway looked and sounded terrifying. But the boys didn't seem too bothered by this, they were just in awe of the house. The initial contract would be for one year. I didn't notice that there was an internet shop directly outside the compound which didn't bode well for the boys schooling. It was likely to end up competing with their video game addiction.

We went back to "The Triangle" to get some food. I decided to treat Paul's entire extended family to a late lunch in Jollibee. There were around ten of us and for some reason this seemed to totally confuse the restaurant staff. Various items from our order were missing. When I raised the query, the staff were bickering with each other as to which one of them was going to deal with the discrepancy. They then handed the problem to a further member of staff who obviously had no idea what the problem was or that he was being stitched up by his colleagues. He dutifully approached us with a view to taking our order again. After explaining again that items from our original order were missing this member of staff asked for our receipts. Irritatingly, he refused to take our word for it and insisted on checking everything off by thoroughly searching our tables. He looked at us suspiciously and checked all around the area as if we might have hidden the items. In the end, he also passed our order to someone else, who stood at a distance for a while, probably summoning the courage to approach us again.

I lost my patience in the end partly because I didn't want to be forced to camp in Olongapo for the night. I stood up and loudly said "Look we are missing a spaghetti dish and one coke, please can someone just get it for us." Then, there was the customary "Ok Ma'am," before the man who had been lurking realised I was addressing him, and disappeared to get the items. In the Philippines, the customer isn't always right.

Grandma liked the house although I think she would have preferred something smaller. She was somewhat embarrassed by what appeared to her to be a luxurious living situation. Having chatted to the landlady and politely but firmly removed some large Catholic posters of Jesus that donned the walls, we agreed some basic rules and paid a deposit and one-month rental. Having promised the world and having set out to deliver, I suddenly realised that I was completely out of cash. I didn't even have sufficient to pay for my return journey to Cubao so was reduced to begging my parents in England to send some emergency funds via Western Union. The initial response from my father that the delivery might be delayed due to his computer hard-drive having been struck by lightning might seem like a handy excuse, but happened to be true. I watched the clock, as visions of the drunken bunch that made up the "Triangle folk" loomed large in my mind. Ministering to them was one thing, sharing benches and concrete steps, even just for one night was definitely undesirable. I was relieved when the money arrived and I just managed to catch the last bus back to Cubao by standing in its path as it was leaving the station!

CHAPTER TWENTY-THREE

Grandma Goes Rogue

The basic simple rules from the landlady, which also suited our purposes were an 11pm curfew and no overnight guests. The boys also knew that they were obviously not allowed to take drugs or solvents, drink alcohol or smoke. They were both enrolled in school, were expected to attend their classes and to generally behave themselves.

Problems began immediately—they spent their entire week's food budget in one splash on "essential cooking utensils." Paul produced receipts which was the only saving grace. I had known that there would be teething problems and that flexibility would be required. But, after just another couple of days, I received a somewhat garbled message that Grandma had left the house for the street leaving the boys unsupervised and declaring her firm resolve never to return. I had no idea *why* this had happened because Paul was unable to communicate the reason, beyond the fact that she had left after an argument. Our extremely confusing conversation included the words "big house", "grandma," "leave" and "cradle." Clearly, it wasn't going to be something that I could sort out from a distance.

Returning to Olongapo, I located Grandma and several of Paul's other relatives sleeping on some cardboard on the street. She didn't seem angry or upset which was the first possible hurdle out of the way. I invited her for coffee to discuss the situation, hoping to lure her away from the various relatives who were also likely wanting to relocate to more pleasant accommodation.

This may sound like a harsh judgement, but the reality was that in helping one family or in this case two former rugby boys, it would have been very easy to have ended up with twenty other people trailing around after me. The tough thing was that most of them did really need help, but it was important to focus on one person or family at a time and not to become overwhelmed by the need. During this particular trip, members of Paul's family asked me what I was going to do for them. In response, I asked how they had been supporting themselves before I came along. Obtaining the answer, I advised them to continue doing what they had been doing before. I knew it wasn't what they had been hoping for, and I did feel that I may have appeared less than sympathetic at times.

Grandma agreed to join me for "coffee" but after I had managed to free her from the loiterers, she changed the destination to "Jollibee" en route. This would be similar to an old lady in England asking to go to McDonalds or Burger King instead of a posh coffee shop. Once inside, I realised the reason for her request as on giving her one hundred pesos (about one pound fifty) she proceeded to use her Senior Citizens discount to buy several burgers and other items to take out. I was hoping I wasn't going to have to grab hold of her as she raced out of the door to distribute the items that clearly were not for her personal consumption. I wondered if she even remembered the reason why I had invited her for coffee. Apparently, I had underestimated her though, as she collected her change and passed it straight to me before calmly agreeing to accompany me upstairs for our chat.

It appeared the argument had been about food money as they had run out prior to the expected date. It seemed we had made a rather drastic miscalculation as to their needs. I had asked one local family how much they spent on food a week and used this to calculate a budget. But I was later informed by another family that they spent double that amount per day that the first family spent per week!

Having dealt with one half of the dispute, I went to the house and surprisingly found both of the boys there in the middle of the day. I had expected them to be at school but, apparently, they had a free day. Several of Paul's relatives that weren't meant to be living there were also hanging around as if waiting for me to leave.

Discussing the conflict with the boys, I detected elements of deception in relation to some of the smaller aspects of how they had spent the household budget. I had been half expecting this. Despite the behavioural changes in the boys, they had still originated from the street, it would take them time to learn basic things like the importance of complete honesty. It was really quite funny as they seemed unaware that they were blatantly and obviously contradicting each other. They apparently couldn't remember things they had allegedly done just hours before and gave vague answers to my questions.

I wasn't prepared to let it go. Knowing the two boys well, I took a chance and played them off against each other. Paul finally admitted that he had gambled some money on a machine and won, and he had then used the additional money to buy a cell phone. The revelation explained the nice new phone with a camera that I had immediately seen lurking in the kitchen area on my arrival. I had already been somewhat suspicious when none of the legitimate residents wanted to claim it as their own. I pointed out that my cell phone didn't even have a camera at which point Paul offered to swap! There were still elements of their story that didn't add up, but Paul was beginning to get upset. Realising what the problem was, in the end I asked him "Did you lie because you didn't want me to know you had gambled?" Immediately he answered "yes." I left some of the more minor details at this point, and told the boys to get ready as we were going out.

Sometimes, I had to give the boys a way out and not back them into a corner. I felt that I had got as close as I was going to get to the truth. On the street, the boys had learned never to tell tales on each other. It was one of the things that stayed with them if they left the street as it was so deeply ingrained. For this reason, outsiders may never really get the complete truth down to the last detail. The boys might even have been covering for someone who appeared to have had no connection to the events. I learned to take what I could get from them, seeing each admission of guilt and apology as a step forward, and then to move on.

I took the opportunity to ask the boys to cease contacting me in Manila, usually via social networking sites, whenever they had problems or issues. I reminded them that they were not eight years old and needed to learn how to resolve conflict themselves. That if they got upset with each other they should go for a walk to calm down then go home, sit down and talk about it. Under no circumstances should they storm out threatening not to come back. Of course, the boys astutely pointed out that it was Grandma and not them who had done this. I advised them, much to their delight, that I had already informed Grandma that she was not to do this again. It wouldn't normally be appropriate in Filipino culture for a younger person to issue directions to someone older, but as a foreigner I could sometimes cautiously say things that a local person wouldn't be able to.

Leaving the house, I arranged a rendezvous with Grandma to ensure the problem was resolved and that they could all live happily ever after (well at least for one year until the house contract expired.) At this point my Britishness came into its own as I loudly said to them all, with friends present, "Okay, are we all friends again, no more problems? No need for me to come rushing back to Olongapo any time soon?" There was an embarrassed silence as I shoved Paul's shoulder to get him to admit that actually he did love his grandma, resulting in a big toothless grin. Then Joel without prompting said that he also loved her so we were all good to go. Take two!

CHAPTER TWENTY-FOUR

Evicted!

After just a few weeks of independence, the boys had somehow ended up attending a Catholic church and a cult church (Iglesia Ni Cristo). How this had happened was beyond me as everything had been in place for them to attend a Bible believing Christian church on both Sundays. There had been some confusion over dress codes and the boys thinking that Grandma couldn't attend a "born again" church because she wasn't "born again."

Additionally, Simon, another of my former "rugby boys", had at last been released from rehab. Paul and Joel cheerfully informed me that Simon was now staying at the house thinking I would be pleased that another of their number was "going straight." However, I hadn't seen evidence of a sincere desire to change in Simon as I had in the other boys. Our charity had also funded the reconstruction of Simon's own home with his disabled father in preparation for his release. So, more than anything, I was frustrated.

For an unknown reason, Grandma then took to the streets again. I heard rumours from several sources that boys other than Paul and Joel were staying with them. Also, that Joel was not attending school and was using solvents again. I was devastated and surprised when Paul broke a golden rule about telling tales and confirmed that Joel, Simon and other boys were using solvents.

Returning once more to Olongapo, I located Grandma who confirmed that she no longer wanted to reside at the rented house. She preferred to sleep on the street as she had been doing before my intervention. The root of the problem was that she wanted to be able to house members of her extended family and was upset that it wasn't allowed. She had effectively thrown the baby out with the bathwater and was stomping her feet in protest.

I decided that I had to take decisive action to prevent the boys using the house as a solvent haven and to protect Paul from the influence of his friends. Reporting his best friend like this was a very tough thing for Paul to do and was virtually unheard of in the street-world. I had always told the boys that if they tried to do what was right I would meet them halfway and help them. Although I knew that Paul had probably also made mistakes I could tell that he was trying to do what was right despite being surrounded by family and friends who were making no effort whatsoever.

I went to the house to put an end to the most disastrous project in the history of mission work. I discovered Joel, Simon and one other small, unfamiliar boy, Ramiro, asleep upstairs. Paul was awake and seemed prepared for the inevitable. I offered him a final opportunity to get away from the temptations of his old life by returning with me to live at my church in Cubao on a temporary basis. He was worried about his family so I outlined my ideas for their continued support to try and put his mind at ease. Reassured, he finally agreed that he would leave with me later in the day, but first, I needed to deal with the rebels.

After talking briefly to the other boys. I told them all to leave detailing the evidence I had gathered that they were using solvents. Joel tried to deny it but then admitted that he had been using a solvent. He half-heartedly argued that he had thought it wouldn't count as it wasn't actually "rugby," it was a different solvent. I had apparently made the mistake of specifying that they shouldn't use "rugby" rather than solvents in general. It was a terribly weak and flawed argument and Joel knew it. I ended the conversation abruptly.

The three evictees mocked me as they packed up their things. Joel took great delight in dramatically removing his school books and uniform from his bag. He dumped them unceremoniously on the floor at our feet with a loud crash, signalling his future intentions not to attend his classes. I knew that he was trying to hurt me because I was the one who had been insisting that they went to school. The tragic reality was that he was only hurting himself by throwing away his education. The noisy trio began leaving the house. I endured the taunting and hostility in shocked silence, but couldn't resist telling them, in a firm but resigned tone, that I would see them back in rehab. Their derisive laughter spoke volumes but I knew that ultimately this was where they would end up, again.

Knowing their future destination, I felt no measure of satisfaction, only a deep sadness at the ruined lives that had shown promise for a time. I was particularly upset by Joel's behaviour as I had been sure that he was sincere in his desire to change. I also felt great frustration towards a system that had allowed Simon to leave rehab halfway through a school year, but that had not allowed him to resume his education outside the institution. I was convinced that had Simon been usefully occupied, things would have been so very different. His influence on the others began the downward spiral for Joel. He had been drawn back into his old circle of friends by Simon who, through no fault of his own, didn't have anything better to do with his time.

After the three boys had left, Paul and I stood in sober silence for a few seconds as we recovered from the confrontation. I had the additional burden of the knowledge that I had just made three teenagers homeless. Paul was no doubt worrying about the welfare of his family as he was about to leave for Cubao. I then prepared myself for what I knew must come next.

I had been dreading dealing with the landlady who had by this point endured a lot more than was reasonable without complaint. She had even tried to help the boys in some ways by offering them advice and small change when they had run out of money. I felt terrible having offered such clear reassurances to her just a few weeks earlier. I was thankful that she didn't blame me for what had subsequently happened. She still seemed to be grateful that I had attempted to help the boys despite the arrangement having failed. She saw the boys almost as her cultural responsibility more than they were mine.

We came to an agreement about the contract and I think she was most likely relieved that the boys were moving on. She remarked that it had been a refreshing change to meet people who genuinely wanted to help others as she didn't come across many that really cared. I was encouraged that at least my Christian witness to her had remained intact despite what had happened. I gave her a copy of my book about the ministry to the boys and told her the code names of the boys that she had been half-supervising. She was very excited and wanted my autograph which I reluctantly gave due to the circumstances.

Paul carried his own mattress and pillow to the bus stop and we left straight away for Cubao in the hope that we wouldn't arrive too late at night. Transferring one or other of the boys to Cubao temporarily had been a possibility for some time. I knew that one or other of them might need to be separated from the unhelpful influence of their street friends. I did feel a bit worried knowing that Paul was technically still a juvenile, but I really didn't see an alternative. He was willing and my church charity had agreed to house him. I went ahead with trepidation believing that God would guide us longer term.

CHAPTER TWENTY-FIVE

Milestones

I was now technically responsible for Paul who by most accounts was aged sixteen, although paperwork had at one stage emerged suggesting he was actually eighteen. Regardless, even if the latter proved to be true, Paul wasn't your average eighteen-year-old having lived his formative years on the street abusing solvents with his peers.

We arrived at the bus terminal in Cubao in the evening and decided to try and grab a taxi due to all of Paul's worldly belongings being in tow. I tried to avoid the line of men attempting to escort people to taxis for a price when the taxis were already lined up waiting for customers. I dodged around one such man to flag down a taxi which was sitting in the centre of the road with a bus waiting impatiently behind it. We piled into the taxi without much pre-planning and I ended up squashed underneath Paul's mattress and pillow in the back of the car as Paul got in the front with the driver. Obviously, Paul had no idea where we were going and as I tried to mumble directions through the material, I was really more concerned that I couldn't see whether the driver had switched on the meter. We were definitely back in Manila.

We arrived at my church in the middle of the anniversary for the drop-in which was a bit chaotic. The people were in the process of fighting over various gift items that the staff had hung from the ceiling on metal railings. The bars were gradually lowered towards the waiting throng who were expected to jump and grab the attached items and pull them from the bars. The problem was that the people were so desperate for whatever was in the packages that actual fights were breaking out and some were always injured. I also felt that it turned the people who were obviously materially poor already into animals biting and scratching to get what they wanted. I had raised my concerns about this "game" in the past, but as it was a Filipino thing I had to leave it at that. After the game, the hundreds of people were seated to view photos from previous drop-in years on a big screen, before being assembled for chaotic group photos.

Despite the mayhem, I eventually managed to find someone who could help Paul settle in at the half-way house attached to my church. Paul would be sharing the house with a small group of men of different ages most of whom had originated from poor backgrounds and one who had come from the street. They were all involved in the church and I was hoping they would be a good influence on Paul spiritually, although not all of them had made professions of faith.

The next day, I enrolled Paul in the Alternative Learning System, a government programme which offered limited hours for students that had missed a lot of school. We also visited a local dentist and began Paul's dental treatment. I had been promising to help him get his teeth sorted out for a long time as he had lost all of the front ones due to decay. Whilst in Cubao, after numerous appointments and extractions, he was finally fitted with dentures which made him look like a different person!

Paul was offered a great opportunity to be an apprentice car spray painter full time. He would be employed by one of our church deacons who owned the business. The wages were low but I could subsidise them and Paul would learn a trade that he could use in the future. I probably didn't think enough about whether Paul would be up to the task having never had any type of paid employment. I also didn't really consider whether placing him in an environment with the strong smell of paint would be wise.

Paul's move to Cubao began to be viewed as something of a test case. If he settled down, stuck at his job and integrated into the church community, then other former "rugby boys" from the rehab centre or from Olongapo might be able to follow in his footsteps. My ultimate goal was still to have some kind of facility for them but I had learned to take small steps of faith. It did feel like a lot was riding on Paul's shoulders because he was now the only boy from our original ministry that had actually remained off the street and off the solvents. I began to place a lot of hope in him as an individual. In a perverse way, I suppose I believed that as long as Paul's profession of faith and the changes in his life continued to appear to be genuine, then the ministry I had been doing was worthwhile. I started to measure my success as a missionary by Paul's progress forgetting that God controlled results and that success isn't defined in terms of numbers. I was about to be knocked off this precarious perch in a painful way.

On what was meant to be Paul's first day at his new spray painting job, he instead arrived at my house early in the morning. Apparently, the jeepney that he was meant to catch hadn't turned up. Paul was meant to wait at the end of the road and then to try to find a space on the impossibly full jeepney. Being young and relatively thin he could in theory jump onto the back, and then hang off the roof whilst standing on the step which is what a lot of the men did. Still half asleep I mumbled something about taking a different jeepney halfway and then transferring. Ideally, he needed to work some of these issues out for himself if he was to survive in the world of work.

Maybe my initial confidence in his ability had been misplaced. Paul did manage to catch a different jeepney but then ended up completely lost and some distance away. Somehow whilst lost, he saw the only person, aside from church members, that he probably knew in the entire area of tens of thousands of people. Unfortunately, he knew the person, a bi-sexual tattoo artist in his late thirties, from rehab. They had mixed the adults and children together at times, a bad idea from any perspective. Having left rehab, the man had continued taking hard drugs. On randomly sighting Paul in the street, he had promptly invited him back to his house, where he had offered him a paid job driving trucks. Paul had declined the offer but didn't know how to get back to Cubao.

He had eventually resorted to contacting me via Facebook to explain why he hadn't turned up for work. I was mortified by the turn of events and couldn't help suspecting that Paul would succumb to the temptation of his former vices being suddenly surrounded by them. I couldn't really understand how he had managed to "bump" into the man in the first place. I told him to return to Cubao immediately by any possible means, praying that he would take the sensible path and do so. To my relief, Paul did arrive sometime later looking a bit sheepish. I was so pleased to see him sober and drug and tattoo free after his bizarre detour that any lecture I might have been preparing went out of the window.

I accompanied him to work on the following day even though it involved getting up ridiculously early. I didn't want to risk him getting lost again and meeting another of his wayward friends. Having completed his first day on the job he turned up at my house that evening looking worse for wear and totally exhausted. He also looked unhappy. He said that it had been really very hard. He described how the fumes from the paint spray had made him feel sick and had given him a headache. I was already aware that he suffered from serious travel sickness the minute he set foot on any vehicle and that he needed to take a daily tablet to combat it. He had forgotten to take his pills, which was something else that he would need to take personal responsibility for.

I was worried realising that he needed to be eased into working full time having been used to a life of leisure. I was also wondering whether his long-term health problems might affect his ability to work in these conditions. I began to think that it probably wasn't an ideal place for him to work. The paint fumes must've been quite similar to the solvent smell that Paul had been addicted to in the past. It was almost like putting him in the path of serious temptation day in and day out. But the possibility of landing him a job with no requirements as he had literally stepped foot in Cubao, had seemed almost too good to be true.

He turned up after his second day on the job looking much more cheerful so I started believe it could work. He had become lost again on his way to work and had contacted me. I had made it clear that he must try and get to work. I had prayed for him and hoped he wouldn't abandon his attempts and give up completely. He said he had been feeling desperate knowing that he must get to work if he wanted to keep his job. After circling around in different jeepneys and asking people for directions for a while he had almost given up hope. He had begun looking for a jeepney back to Cubao, and as his desperation increased had even considered heading back to Olongapo. He felt just so fed up and discouraged, but had suddenly thought that maybe he should pray. When he opened his eyes having done so, he was literally right outside his work place. He enthusiastically jumped off the jeepney and headed straight to work. The answered prayer had also helped him mentally as he had realised that God really did want him to have the job. He had resolved therefore to try again and make it work.

Unfortunately, his resolution only lasted a matter of weeks. He "lost" his entire first week's wages. I struggled to believe his story at first, but he maintains to this day that he actually did lose the money. He subsequently became very ill at work and began vomiting. He ended up lying down on a couch for the rest of his shift one day. He wasn't physically able to do the work required of him. Finally, I realised that he wouldn't be able to continue and that he would need to find other work. I knew this would be virtually impossible due to his lack of education and official paperwork identification.

The influences in the work place had also been bad for him as the other workers were not Christians. The church leader who owned the business and had given him the job, wasn't there a lot of the time due to other commitments. Paul was therefore on his own with a load of older men who were very much living in the world. He felt the pull of his old life and started to ask if he could go and play basketball with the men from work. I had reluctantly given permission wanting him to make friends. I had been hoping that he would gravitate more towards the men in my church.

On reflection, a combination of factors probably meant that his first paid job was doomed from the outset. It was a long way away requiring travel on public transport, he was working with solvents, the staff were non-believers and he wasn't being paid enough to live on. It was definitely time for a rethink.

We were also still having the odd blip where Paul fell into deliberate sin as he worked out his relationship with God. I discovered one day that he had been secretly saving money that I had been giving him for food and had bought an expensive cell phone with it. It seemed that Paul's desire for a flashy cell phone would get him into trouble on more than one occasion. I wouldn't have been that bothered but he had often come to our door begging for food on the basis that his allowance wasn't enough and that he was hungry.

When I had proved the lie, he produced the phone on demand and I confiscated it, only returning it some-time later as a gift. The item had become tainted with guilt by then and Paul seemed reluctant to receive it which was an interesting change of attitude. He had told me that his friend with the tattoos that he had bumped into that day had given him most of the money for it. But he admitted using food money that I had given him to make up the amount required. I felt we were making progress as Paul saw being caught as evidence that God was watching him and that his sin would always find him out in the end.

CHAPTER TWENTY-SIX

Ramiro: Too Young to Die

Job issues and the occasional bad choice aside, Paul was starting to settle down in Cubao and to become more involved in my church. He even volunteered at the drop-in, helping prepare food for the homeless people. My heart leapt every-time I saw him sitting in the congregation at the meetings. There were those who made an effort to befriend him, although some were not so willing. However, he regularly mentioned that he missed his relatives and friends in Olongapo and couldn't wait for the visit that I had promised him.

Paul was different to the mainstream people that he was now mixing with and he knew it. He often confided to me that he felt people didn't like him. My reassurances were not always enough and weren't entirely honest because I knew that sadly in some cases he was right. When he sinned, they sometimes gossiped instead of offering a loving rebuke. Several times he packed his bags and headed off for Olongapo. We even got as far as the bus station one day, but eventually he heeded my warnings about the temptations of his former life if he went back before he was ready. He was ashamed to tell me that he had reversed his decision so just disappeared from the terminal, leaving all of his belongings on the ground for me to deal with. I tolerated this type of behaviour as I knew he was confused and trying to find his place in life and in his faith. I prayed that a day would arrive when he fitted in, but knew from experience that it would be a tough ask.

I had seen it happen before in Christian circles, especially those with a conservative worldview. Someone that has led a rough life feels that they are different—they have different life experiences and cannot see the world in the same way. They make assumptions about regular Church attendees that quite often are completely inaccurate. They believe that they are so far beneath these people that they will never live up to expectations and will always fail. Unfortunately, often Christians don't do much to correct the stereotypes in the person's mind. They may say that they are unworthy sinners too, but the former street person doesn't really believe it—they haven't seen it and as far as they are concerned, the other Christians are clothed in white with a halo because most of their sin is invisible. Revealing some personal sin can help to combat the error as it can help the person understand the reality that we are all unworthy sinners and on a level playing field before a holy God. This is why the testimony of someone who has lived a worldly life can be so powerful as others who are struggling can relate to them.

Then came the tragic news that I had been dreading since the beginning of my ministry with the "rugby boys." One of the Olongapo boys had died in an accident with a jeepney. Sadly, Ramiro, aged fourteen was one of the boys I had evicted from the failed housing project. If I hadn't seen him again after the eviction I think I would've been overcome by guilt that my last memory of him was such a horrible one. I don't think it would have mattered that he shouldn't have been there in the first place and that the other boys knew this. I think it just would've been a terrible memory.

By God's grace, I had seen the evictees again, a few hours after the eviction, before Paul and I had left Cubao. It was Ramiro that I had seen first, he was standing watching me as Paul and I looked for a place to eat. I recognised him and as I had recovered from the stress of the earlier events I asked him if he was hungry. He of course said that he was and suddenly Joel, Simon and another boy appeared. I invited them all to eat with us and only Joel had an internal battle with his pride before accepting help from someone that had just made him homeless.

We went to Wimpy and Ramiro sat next to me. We thanked God for the food and I spent most of the meal talking to a Filipino friend as the boys talked amongst themselves. They ordered large steak meals. Ramiro was a small boy and couldn't eat all his food so I asked if he wanted to take it out for later and he said "yes." All of the boys thanked me as they left and that was my last memory of Ramiro.

Just a few days later he died. I was informed that he habitually played around on the jeepneys doing dangerous stunts and activities. This didn't help me to accept what had happened. I had to believe that God had a plan even in death and I hoped and prayed that Ramiro had heard about Jesus. I wrongly assumed that I would see him again and would have the chance to build a relationship with him as I had done with the other boys.

It was the second time someone that I had just met had died within days. Isaac's father had died just a few days after I met him in the rehab where we were both visiting his son. It was a tough lesson but reminded me that I should always find ways to share the Gospel with every person that I met because none of us is guaranteed tomorrow.

Joel and Simon were devastated by the death of Ramiro who they had known since childhood. The frailty of life had been brought close to home and in a private conversation with Joel he admitted that he wasn't happy with his street life. He looked into my eyes and said, "It's very hard to change my life." I knew that it would be impossible if he didn't ask God to help him.

The enemy actively attacked Paul through his Olongapo friends who cruelly tried to use Ramiro's death and his (Paul's) father's declining health to try and get him to return to Olongapo. But, helpfully the homeless people's Bible study on the Monday, was on that very subject. The leader explained how the enemy tries to disrupt our lives when we are trying to change and adapt to a new God given situation. Paul smiled to himself as he acknowledged that God was speaking directly to him.

Paul then made a definite decision to remain in Cubao so I asked one of the pastor's about whether he could be baptised as he had requested. It seemed as though Paul's conversion was genuine and that his move to Cubao had been a success. It also appeared that our test case had been proven and that other "rugby boys" might soon be able to join us in Cubao.

However, God's ways are not our ways as I was about to learn the hard way. The half-way house that Paul was using was owned by Christian Compassion Ministries. His stay had initially been agreed on a temporary basis. CCM suddenly decided that they could no longer accommodate Paul due to his age, lack of documentation and the fact that he hadn't been born in Cubao. My attempts to find solutions failed. Having told Paul that he could stay in Cubao and having spent the past three months convincing him that this was in his best interests. I would now be forced to completely reverse my advice and take him back to Olongapo.

It was with a heavy heart that I accompanied him having tried to explain the reasons, which honestly, I didn't fully understand myself. Paul was crying especially when we reached Olongapo and I had to leave him with his family on the street. He had assumed that I was planning to house them again, but there was no way I could risk it after what had happened before.

Returning alone to Cubao, I tried to switch off my emotions knowing there was nothing I could do about it. I had attempted to reason with the CCM leaders to no avail. They were worried about the law in relation to minors and there had been no men in the church willing to live with Paul independently even temporarily. He couldn't live in our girl's house. There was nothing else that could be done.

A Christian church in Olongapo had been taking an interest in the boys for a number of months. I basically handed over responsibility for them to this church. The members were kind, they even visited Paul's family on the street and persuaded them to attend services.

Despite the church's efforts, Paul returned to his old crowd of street friends and later spent time in prison. I was forced to let go of the misguided notion that somehow my success or failure as a missionary depended on his progress or lack of it. Maybe this was the lesson that God was trying to teach me, to force me to let go of my pride and to give Him the glory instead of trying to keep some for myself. The fiasco with Paul certainly did the trick and broke my heart in many ways.

It was some time after when the wounds had partially healed that I received a small piece of encouragement from a different source, Joel sent me this message on social media.

"I am doing Ok, I am currently studying in ALS (Alternative Learning System) and residing at the Youth Centre. My family is doing well. I asked for forgiveness to Jesus Christ and to you too. How are you Ma'am Natalie? I am deeply sorry for all the bad things I did to you. I know it is hard to restore the trust. Thank you for all the love that you have given us. Someday you will see me doing good in life and I will never forget the love you have shown me."

CHAPTER TWENTY-SEVEN

A Brief Respite

I busied myself with ministry and tried hard not to allow the bitterness I felt over what had happened to the "rugby boys" ministry to seep into my heart. It had been unfair in some ways to expect my church to consider taking on such a huge commitment. I was new to the church, a foreigner and they were already involved in so many activities. Paul's stay at the church may have made them realise what they would be taking on and maybe it had been unrealistic to expect the project to work. The fact that the decision had been taken out of my hands made things easier for me —God had allowed it to happen, I had to accept it and move on.

I heard in 2015 that the Logos Hope ship would be visiting the Philippines again. I had expected it to be four or five years before they re-visited. Initially, Subic Bay wasn't included in the list of proposed ports probably because there was a time when many of us, as crew members, felt as if we lived there due to the extended dry dock in 2012. I was pleased when the schedule was changed to include my former place of residence and began making plans to visit.

On the Saturday, I woke up later than planned and really wasn't in the mood for the long bus journey. I walked to the bus station grabbing take-away breakfast at MCD's en route. I saw several buses travelling in the direction I needed to go and one of them had the signboard for Subic Bay. It also had the SCTEX label which in English terms means "faster bus" due to the route it takes. I was happy to see this bus and flagged it down only to be told that it was full. Why the drivers stop when the bus is already full I couldn't tell you—maybe because they are being polite or because I'm a foreigner.

I was reduced to begging the conductor to let me on the bus and after a few seconds he told me it was standing room only which I agreed to as I didn't want to wait in the bus terminal for hours. I felt a bit embarrassed as I boarded with my coffee in one hand and MCD's takeaway in the other. I normally try not to appear too Westernised avoiding things like Starbucks/Smartphones which Filipino's spend their limited money on. There isn't really a concept of saving money in the Philippines, so many Filipino's use half a day's wages just to buy an expensive coffee rather than the very cheap option from the street vendor or supermarket. I think it's more of a status symbol than anything else judging by the numerous Facebook and Instagram selfies of Filipino's holding their coffee. But, being of a mind-set where cheaper is ALWAYS better even though I did have money to spend, I struggled with the spending habits of many who really couldn't afford to live as they did.

I braced myself for the usual open stares as I looked for a floor space in the centre aisle. This was not the "done thing" from a Filipino perspective as most of them tended to treat Westerners a little like royalty yet here I was unashamedly begging for a bus space and then was about to sit on the dirty floor of a public bus to eat my breakfast. There was a scrambling motion at the front of the bus as the conductor found me a small plastic seat. I gratefully sat down feeling quite hot and bothered and tucked into my burger getting ketchup everywhere in the process. This part was the easy bit as it turned out. Have you ever tried making coffee whilst sitting on the floor of a moving bus in Manila? My big mistake, I took the lid off the coffee before opening the sugar and creamer. The result; coffee everywhere and a burnt hand. Undeterred I tried again and again, becoming increasingly amazed that despite the many local people staring at my predicament no one offered to help me! Eventually I was successful and drank my coffee without further incident. I spent most of the three-hour bus journey standing as it was just too uncomfortable to sit down and in the last fifteen minutes a kind man offered me his seat.

As we reached the Harbour Point shopping mall in Olongapo where we had previously stocked a mini version of the Logos Hope Book-Fair, a strange feeling of nostalgia flooded over me. As it was very hot I approached a taxi rank, taking number two in the line as number one tried to rip me off. Being dropped off about a five-minute walk from where the ship was docked I could only see the very top of the ship with the familiar logo. I felt excited and apprehensive as I walked towards the ship and was greeted by various Book-Fair staff who didn't know that I was ex-crew. Happy to remain anonymous I paid the small entrance fee and began wandering towards the visitor's gangway only to be recognised by the personnel manager Dan who happened to be coming down the crew gangway. This was the first of many hugs. I had forgotten about the hugging culture on Logos Hope which I had just about adjusted to after two years on-board. I spent the following two years re-adjusting as I like my personal space!

Hug and questions over, I met up with Arlene, a former ship-mate, who was also visiting for a few days. This was when things got very surreal as we headed for our favourite seats in the dining room. I'm guessing that the crazy people who had extended their commitment beyond our time on board, thought they were in some kind of time capsule as they saw us sitting there again. I poured myself some of the powdered lemon juice drink and chatted with a number of people feeling very odd and kind-of out of place, but everyone was very friendly. Then we headed down to the Book-Fair where I had previously worked as administrator.

Next, we went to the International Café (I-cafe) where I had also worked when first on-board. I thought back to the many conversations with visitors in different countries and some of the incidents that had taken place amongst the staff. I recalled a water-bomb fight using a blown-up plastic glove that exploded on hitting its target. Also, the many times that less capable crew members had poured the heavy ice cream mix over the top and side of the machine when refilling instead of into it, resulting in the machine coming to an abrupt standstill and beeping loudly in protest, as thousands of people waited not-so-patiently in line.

The ship seemed eerily quiet during our visit and I asked Arlene whether she had also noticed the silence and whether it had been like this when we were on-board. It seemed to me that it had always been relatively noisy and full of life and activity especially in the more public areas. On reflection, I realised that the ship hadn't changed but the people had. Most of my friends had moved on and as it was the people that had made the experience, it felt strangely wrong without them. I was really glad at this point that I hadn't booked to stay on-board as I think it would've made me feel very alone and nostalgic.

Arlene had to get back to Manila for a church meeting in the evening so we planned to leave after just a few hours. One of the nicest things about the visit was the great sense of freedom I felt as I walked around knowing that I could stay for as long as I liked *and* leave whenever I wanted. It may sound a bit odd, but towards the end of my time on the ship, I felt a little like I was in a prison, just because I couldn't leave, as I was determined to finish my commitment. Many of those who had joined at the same time as me had left early so the last few months had been especially tough.

By chance (or God) an American lady with a very nice, spacious, air conditioned car happened to be heading back to Manila as we were leaving and offered us a lift. So, we travelled back to Manila in comparative luxury. Arlene was planning several further revisits to Logos Hope during the ship's stay in the Philippines. But, I decided that one visit was enough.

CHAPTER TWENTY-EIGHT

Tacloban Typhoon

Most people will remember the massive typhoon that hit the Philippines in November 2013. It was the deadliest typhoon ever to hit the country and over six thousand people were killed. I had originally been intending to travel to the Philippines at around the time the storm hit but had been delayed by a few weeks. I watched the calamity unfold on British TV, staring in shock at the harsh, crazy weather and the resultant flood waters. Then later at the zombie-like survivors wandering the flattened, barren land searching for food. It could've been a movie, it seemed that far removed from reality in the West. Had I been there, I would no doubt have been overwhelmed by the many and various needs and become paralysed in my inability to make effective decisions. In short, any help I might have been able to offer would've been as a drop in an ocean from the beach at high tide.

A year or so after the disaster, the mass clean-up was still taking place in Tacloban, one of the areas that had been most severely affected. My church decided to take a team in a couple of vans to provide medical help and to attempt to share the Gospel in the area. The journey would take around twenty-eight hours, which is a long time squashed in a van with relief goods and personal belongings.

On arrival, the first thing that hit me was the stifling heat. We had been warned about it but nothing can really prepare a person for such a drastic temperature change and don't forget that I had been living in Manila which easily hits forty degrees in the summer. Tacloban was even hotter and the heat was dry. I felt irritable pretty quickly especially when I discovered that some people had flown to the location avoiding the uncomfortable van ride.

However, the cross-water vehicle ferry was enjoyable even though we had to wait several hours for it. We sang karaoke—a favourite Filipino pursuit. One of the men commented "Oh, you *can* sing." I wasn't sure whether or not this was a compliment as it depended on whether or not he had heard me sing before.

Whilst we were standing on the deck, teenage street boys shouted for us to throw our loose change into the water near the harbour. They then dived down to retrieve it sometimes with their mouths, emerging with the metal glinting between their teeth. In some ways, it sickened me to see comparatively rich people tossing coins to the performers as they entertained for the small money that would purchase their daily needs. But, on the other hand, they needed the cash. It was just the attitude that often went along with the giving—as if these boys were animals on demand for the enjoyment of the foreigners, rather than people, desperately hungry, and often addicted to drugs.

Ministry wise, we had partnered with several local doctors who unfortunately turned out not to be Christians. At the first location, we had all the potential patients lined up and then saw them one by one in their order of arrival. They had to stand in the heat for hours and many didn't understand the queueing system and ended up going around in circles or being duped by their cunning and less charitable neighbours. We took personal details, weight, temperature and a medical history from each patient before sending them to a nurse or doctor for prescriptions. This all took up a lot of time as you can probably imagine with squirming babies and the language barriers. This time, it wasn't just me who didn't speak the language, none of our team did as the area used a completely different dialect.

The doctors, who as I mentioned were mostly non-believers, didn't appear to enjoy their work. They sat grim-faced as they saw patient after patient. Some went for breaks and returned late, whilst others didn't show up at all. They weren't willing to go the extra mile because they didn't understand the ministry side of the work. I especially remember one old man who had been queuing all day. He finally reached a doctor and shyly tried to explain his problem. She stared at him unsympathetically and then interrupted him loudly in an abrupt manner. She implied that he had wasted his time in even attending. I felt tears forming in my eyes and wanted to erase the memory and the pain in this poor man's heart.

After the first day, I suggested that maybe there was no need to take all of the details from each patient. After all, where was the information actually going to end up? Why did we need a temperature for someone who wasn't complaining of a fever or weight for someone who was? Standardised checks are a Western phenomenon but are rarely effective due to each person's body being different. On this occasion, I think our work was tripled by the unnecessary bureaucracy. Eventually, we did begin to hone in on the symptoms to try and reduce the ever-growing lines and to keep the peace as people became frustrated and dehydrated in the heat.

I took the temperature of one lady who looked a little worse for wear and extremely pale. The result made me balk and I double checked it wondering how she was still functioning. The doctor sent her immediately to hospital in a make-shift ambulance. It was a similar story for a baby I checked later that day. Both patients were okay in the end, well, at least in the short term.

I commented to a fellow worker that I was surprised not to see more serious injuries and illnesses emerging from the crowds of people. Due to the calamity of the typhoon, I had anticipated lines of malnourished, or those who couldn't afford treatment for serious diseases. But, we actually had very few of these types of cases. Most people were there for a basic health check or for coughs and colds. I wondered whether our work had really achieved anything as we were just prescribing aspirin and paracetamol in the main. Those that did have serious health issues would need to be referred to a hospital in any event.

I therefore turned my attention to the evangelistic aspect which was the reason I had joined the relief effort. However, this side of things faced similar hurdles as the loud speaker was ineffective in the open air and it was impossible to get people quiet enough to listen to the speaker. Unfortunately, as the event had been advertised as a medical outreach, very few people came expecting to listen to a message, let alone being prepared to have one forced on them. It just wasn't their priority as they jostled each other in the lines and tried desperately to keep their children out of the blazing heat. Maybe tracts would work instead—people could read them at their convenience and take them away. If only they had been in the right language!

I asked why we weren't making greater efforts with the evangelistic side of things and was told that the donations had been designated specifically for relief work. On venturing further into this, I eventually found out that some of the donors had stated that they did not want their money used for Gospel ministry or even to plant a church in the area. I understand they later changed their minds on being re-approached. But, I was incredulous on hearing this—why would a Christian designate their money for non-Gospel ministry?!

Finding that there was a definite excess of volunteers attempting to work in a tiny space, as tended to be the case in the Philippines, I excused myself and went looking for other ministry opportunities. Seeing the basketball court next to where we were operating, I joined a small group of teenage boys who were hovering around. I braved the heat and started a game with them but my face began to burn immediately. I ended up tying cloth around all the parts of my face that I could reach and wearing sunglasses to protect my eyes. This had the effect of making me feel like I was invisible or at least unrecognisable as I dashed around with the boys for an hour or so in the hottest part of the day.

After we all nearly perished in the heat, I grabbed the boys some water from our table as I shared the Gospel with them using a cheeky boy with a big grin as translator. He happened to be from Manila and spoke Tagalog. I managed to find a few tracts to give them and answered their questions. Some mocked but mostly they were respectful and a local policeman came over to see what I was handing them. He had been standing with a large group of police taking shelter from the heat under a tree. I took the opportunity to tell him that I was formerly a police officer as I handed him and his colleagues tracts. I called a male co-worker over to explain the Gospel to them as well and after initially looking at me as if I was crazy, he joined us and did a great job.

I was encouraged that despite the lack of opportunities during the organised ministry, we were still able to share our faith with some who were eager to hear. But, I had overlooked one essential body part during my frantic cover-up—my ears were burnt to a crisp and began peeling soon after. I didn't know how people could learn to live in these temperatures.

For the long van journey back, I opted to join the guys van assuming they would be less likely to talk at the tops of their voices in a high pitch. Also, that they probably wouldn't be wanting to stop and examine the view every five minutes. I had had enough and just wanted to get back. I determined never again to foolishly think I could handle that long a drive in extreme heat and with that many people. It was a simple lesson in knowing and respecting my personal limitations, something that I have never been very good at!

CHAPTER TWENTY-NINE

Claustrophobic Cages

Another avenue of service that was open to me was to visit and become involved in churches in areas other than Cubao. Grace Ministerial Academy, the Bible school which operated from my church, trained leaders and then sent them out either to pioneer or to lead existing ministries. Many of these eventually formed into actual churches, although it sometimes took a while for them to get the resources to do so. One small church I attended was meeting above a darkened internet shop with kids playing computer games twenty-four-seven whilst waiting for a more suitable building.

Another of these ministries was in a place called Valenzuela about a two-hour drive from Cubao. I really had no idea what I was letting myself in for when I enthusiastically volunteered to assist the small church with a youth activity on Saturday afternoons. The travel involved walking for twenty-five minutes to the MRT station (similar to a train or tram,) catching the MRT for several stops, walking again for fifteen minutes, surviving on a thing called a STEX for over an hour, then catching a jeepney for ten minutes and finally a tricycle to reach the pastor's house. If any of these links malfunctioned or weren't on time then I could be massively delayed or fail to make it at all, which happened several times. It was a day of travelling for a one hour programme, and although I didn't mind if I was needed, I was a little perturbed on learning that the man who "assisted" me with the study had actually been leading it until my arrival.

The STEX is a large car that travels a certain route using basically the same system as a bus except that it remains at the stop until it is full. There are hundreds of cars and hundreds of routes. The drivers attempt to squash as many people as possible into each car until one day I objected to being slotted in between two large Filipino men in the back of the vehicle. I politely but firmly asked if I could wait outside the vehicle until there were enough people to fill it. I thought that some women might arrive and I could sit next to them instead. The driver became belligerent and refused my request suggesting that he might choose to leave me behind. As a foreigner, I didn't often encounter such rudeness from Filipinos but occasionally some who seemed to resent my presence in their country behaved like this.

I recalled one day being on a jeepney but, apparently, my legs were too long. An old lady got very frustrated as she tried to manoeuvre around them as she was getting off the vehicle. She turned around and slapped me hard across the legs in anger whilst muttering something unintelligible to anyone who happened to be listening. I just behaved as if nothing had happened, but everyone else seemed as if they were frozen in time as they waited for my reaction. What was I going to do? Call the police and tell them an eighty plus year old woman just assaulted me because my legs were in her way or nothing, right?

In relation to the STEX, it really didn't make a difference to the driver as he would still have a full car. I managed in the end to fit at the end of a row but my face and body were squashed against the window and side of the car throughout the journey which was stalled by traffic. These journeys were so uncomfortable and the interior of the vehicles claustrophobic with little ventilation. I became a bit panicky one day when we had been sitting in one for hours in the traffic and I couldn't breathe properly. I asked the driver to pull over but he refused as it wasn't a recognised stopping point. Realising I was at breaking point, I begged the other passengers to persuade him to stop but they all just gawped at me. I felt really ill and became desperate to get out of the vehicle which wasn't moving in any event, but the driver refused to allow me to leave. When a fellow passenger eventually took pity on me and swung the door open, the driver ordered it shut and quickly moved the vehicle forward a few metres. I was banging on the windows, and practically crying by the point he finally let me out with no apology. I decided after this day that I had better not ride the STEX again as it was obviously too much for my system to cope with.

The children that attended the youth activities in Valenzuela were from a local slum area. They had to climb over a fence to get to the meeting and sometimes didn't turn up because they had been stopped by the police in the process. We also lost some attendees who decided it was more fun to swim in the dirty river nearby. We played ball games before the short Bible study and then gave them a snack afterwards. Often, we were disrupted by the frequent and heavy rain. Things seemed to conspire against us but we tried to work round the issues rather than giving up. We purchased a large wooden hut for shelter from the rain. It was great until the termites got at it. But we persevered.

Ironically, it was not the police, the river or the weather that put an end to my trips to Valenzuela. The travelling and the fact that there was a male teacher available to teach the mostly male teenagers did it in the end. But not before the slum kids had attended a youth camp run by the local reformed Baptist churches. Unfortunately, the pitch was slightly above their heads but they definitely enjoyed themselves and had been hearing the Gospel for a number of additional months by the time I departed.

CHAPTER THIRTY

Pregnant and Homeless

I tended to get too emotionally involved with individuals sometimes as those who have read my earlier books will recognise. I found it very difficult to separate head from heart and often was frustrated that I couldn't do more practically. Jenny began attending the drop-in and other church ministries. I immediately noticed her because she was heavily pregnant and had a toddler trailing round after her. She appeared to be alone. I befriended her over a few weeks and established that she was living and sleeping on the street due to having been abandoned by her boyfriend. I didn't know that she had a history with my church and she didn't mention it. I believed what she told me but had no way to verify her story.

I approached the church for advice as to what to do to help Jenny and it was suggested that she might be able to be placed in a refuge of some sort whilst she gave birth to her baby. Her other child would be taken into temporary foster care. I didn't like the idea but felt that maybe it was all that could be done for her. Despite the suggestion, nothing was happening and Jenny was getting closer and closer to her due date. I was starting to worry that she would end up having the child alone in a dirty back alley on the street somewhere.

She asked me if I could buy powdered milk for her toddler, and not thinking much of it I gave her the two hundred pesos (around three pounds.) Arriving at church the following week, I was confronted by some church members demanding to know why I had given Jenny money as it was against procedure. Apparently, Jenny had now returned to the church asking for another week's worth of milk due to my lapse in judgement. The leaders were worried about starting trends amongst the homeless that they couldn't keep up. I pointed out that Jenny's situation was somewhat more precarious than the average homeless person and that she was clearly in immediate need. Plus, she had actually spent the money on milk, this fact was not disputed.

A pastor appeared during the discussion, he wanted to know what the church was doing to help Jenny as she was obviously needing our assistance. Several of us began debating her case and how best to help her in what we thought was a private area of the church. Suddenly, in the middle of the discussion, I glanced towards the door and saw Jenny listening and watching everything. She looked distraught. I rushed towards her to explain, but she began apologising profusely thinking she had got me into trouble with the church. I reassured her, but the damage had been done and she left without staying for lunch.

I was really upset and kept crying every time I thought about what had happened. To my mind, Jenny had come to the church seeking help in her greatest hour of need. Regardless of who was at fault we had seriously let her down and made her feel guilty for having asked for help in the first place. I learned from social workers that Jenny had a history of failed relationships and poor life choices which had resulted in her first two children being taken into care. But, I wasn't convinced that the additional information made any difference. Is there a limit to the number of times we should help someone?

Jenny was booked into the hospital to have her baby. Somehow, her mother was notified of her whereabouts and she turned up in Cubao to help her daughter with the toddler and new arrival. What a relief it was to see someone who cared sitting beside Jenny at the drop-in from that day onwards.

I have included this incident to help those considering missionary work to see how tricky some of the situations on the field can be. There was no right or wrong answer or tried and tested solution in Jenny's case. The charity had an inflexible policy that they had to stick to for fear of being inundated with requests. They had probably reached this agreement due to having been more flexible in the past and learning the hard way that the rules needed to be tightened up. I was an inexperienced missionary in a foreign culture but seeking to obey the Biblical instruction to help someone who I saw was in need. I had the capacity to help her and believed I should do so. Yet, I also wanted to submit to the policies of the charity as they were part of my church.

Jenny was helped ultimately by her mother joining her which seemed to have occurred independently of anything either I or the charity had arranged. Her sudden presence reminded me that God was in control and working all things for His glory, maybe we were getting in the way.

CHAPTER THIRTY-ONE

The Bali Conspiracy

I awoke one fine day, sleepily rubbing my eyes as I wandered into the bathroom. I picked up my toothbrush, examined it to check that it hadn't been recently sampled by a cockroach. This had become part of my daily routine ever since I had seen a huge one sitting on the bristles—now I understood why the Filipino's had plastic brush guards. I had thought they were pointless. I squeezed some toothpaste onto the brush and leaned forward to look in the mirror.

Suddenly, the entire concrete sink fell off the wall and smashed into large pieces on the bathroom floor. I didn't have time to wonder what had just happened as the water pipes had obviously been snapped in the process. A huge plume of water was now gushing from two open pipes. I screamed which brought my housemates running, then decided to try and put an end to the crisis having no idea where the water mains tap was. I braved the water which soaked me instantly and eventually managed to stem the flow by turning something that looked like it might put an end to the drama.

I survived the incident with just a few cuts to my feet. I had unconsciously jumped out of the way of the large hazard as it was falling. I turned to my housemate and her mother who was visiting and, seeing their worried looks, burst out laughing. This served me well when a few weeks later the mother put her toast in the microwave for two minutes and nearly set the house on fire. She was terrified of my reaction as the smoke billowed through the rooms. I swiftly reminded her how I had reacted when the sink had come to life, and assured her that I didn't care at all. These things happened.

I decided it was time for a holiday though, as there had been a lot going on and I was finding the cultural adaption tricky. I was very happy when my best friend from England suggested I join her in Bali, Indonesia for a few days. It was planned to be a relaxing break and my first non-ministry holiday for a very long time. I've never been one for travelling around for the sake of it and don't really enjoy touristy things/sight-seeing/spending lots of money but I was looking forward to catching up with Penny and having some time out.

I had trouble booking my flights as my card kept declining for no apparent reason. I even joked that maybe God didn't want me to go to Bali and subsequent events made me wish in many ways that I hadn't forced the door. Having been in Manila for more than six months but less than a year I was aware that I needed to gain exit clearance before leaving the country. However, I had read updated guidance online which suggested that I could obtain such clearance at the airport. A missionary friend told me that she had done this so I prepared the fee for the airport and didn't think much more about it.

On the day of my flight, I took a taxi to terminal two in Manila as per my online booking. On arrival, after waiting in heavy traffic, I saw that all of the sign boards were for the wrong airline. I therefore asked a guard to check whether I was at the correct terminal. This seemed to cause a great deal of confusion as various members of staff tried to assist with my relatively simple question. It took at least fifteen minutes to kind-of confirm that my flight was not due to depart from this terminal but the guard was unwilling to clearly clarify which terminal I was meant to be at only telling me that my airline usually departed from terminal three and four (in completely different locations.) We were already running late due to the traffic so I took a gamble and directed the by-now-pretty-irritated taxi driver to terminal three arriving a bit flustered but otherwise okay.

I rushed into the airport and was relieved to see my flight on the board and the queue of people waiting to check-in. I checked in then headed straight for immigration. The immigration official asked if I had clearance so I handed over the exit fee. The man, looking perplexed, called his supervisor. They were joined by a number of other official looking people who began discussing something a few feet away. I still thought things would be fine and was waiting for them to come back, take the fee and wave me through. But on his return the official told me that they didn't allow clearance at the airport and that I would need to attend the main immigration office which was a number of miles away!

At this point, I began to worry as having been in the Philippines for some years I knew that bureaucratic procedures were not easily negotiated even if they didn't make any sense. I asked to speak to a supervisor and was pointed in the direction of two female supervisors. Neither was particularly helpful and they refused to check online for the updated guidance that I had read. They didn't really listen to what I was saying but just kept pointing to the note in my passport which said that I needed to get exit clearance. After practically begging to be allowed to fly the official informed me that they had already off-loaded me from the flight. I would not be flying to Bali.

Dejected and frustrated I returned to check-in and told a seemingly helpful male staff member what had happened. I asked if it was possible to re-book my flight for later in the day. He said that if I could get to the immigration main office and back within a few hours, I could take a flight later in the afternoon with an onward night flight to Bali arriving the following day in the early hours. He added me as an additional passenger to the already full flight, I thought this was a little odd but didn't question it as it seemed like a lifeline. I rushed out of the airport to try and get a taxi to immigration.

After sitting in traffic for a while I arrived at immigration and made a big fuss about the information on their website not being clear. This seemed to get things moving as I managed to skip the queue. It was then I was told I could in fact get exit clearance at the airport. The staff handed me a note and attached the guidance to present to the officials at the airport. Infuriated, I tried to calm down by thinking of all of the compensation claims I would be making at the conclusion of this fiasco. I'm not one for the compensation culture and suing people left, right and centre, but missing my flight and part of my short holiday due to bureaucratic incompetence was a sacrifice too great.

I grabbed another taxi back to the airport telling myself it wasn't the end of the world and looking forward to my holiday. I arrived breathlessly at check-in to find that of course, the helpful male staff member had gone home. His replacement didn't seem to understand what I was talking about. She told me the flight was already full and that the earliest available flight to Bali was for the following day. I was not booked as an additional passenger on either flight. I showed her the quote and flight details I had received from the male staff member which he has scrawled on a piece of paper. I asked about the night flight that had previously been promised me and was told there was no night flight to Bali!

At this point I became determined to get to Bali that evening. I went around all of the airline desks asking for flights. After being quoted an extortionate price for a one-way ticket, I decided to go and find an internet café to see if I could get it cheaper online. There were no internet cafes or connection in the airport terminal and I didn't have a gadget with WIFI.

I walked out of the terminal and could see some shops down below the ramp where I was standing. I looked around for steps down from the level I was on but couldn't see any. I wandered around for a while and eventually asked someone how to get down to the shops. The man told me I would have to take a taxi as there were no steps. I couldn't believe this, but was too exhausted to argue so got into a taxi and asked the driver to take me to an internet café or shopping area nearby. The driver was old and didn't understand what an internet café was, he also said he didn't know where there were any shops. He was getting stressed by my directions so I got out of the taxi in the middle of nowhere and asked for directions from a random passer-by.

Installed in a café, I found the flight I had been offered earlier at the airport at a cheaper price via Bravofly. It was still painfully expensive but I decided to book it as I could see my holiday plans rapidly fading into obscurity. I was emailed a booking reference but several hours later still had no confirmation. Giving up, I returned to the airport in another taxi to get confirmation directly from the airline. I joined a queue and when I was finally seen I was told that my flight was not confirmed due to an issue with my debit card. Apparently, Bravofly had rejected my order and issued a refund. The airline then suggested I book directly with them, as the ridiculous price they had offered me earlier had apparently been a miscommunication. Relieved, I bought the ticket and prepared myself for the wait for my night flight.

This time I had no problems at immigration and the official even waived part of the exit clearance fee as he couldn't believe what I had already gone through. Arriving at the airport in Bali, I avoided being ripped off by the many taxi drivers. I arrived safely at the hotel and met my friend. After catching up on my sleep for a few hours, we had dinner at a restaurant. The next day we headed into town hoping to make the most of the few days left, but I wasn't feeling quite myself so we returned early. I spent the next two days in bed with food or water poisoning!

On the final day of my holiday and feeling better, I ventured out and we had a good day and a nice meal in the evening. Then I had to get up at 4am for my journey back to the airport. I was forced to hand over double the normal taxi fare due to a mis-arrangement but by this point I really didn't care. At the Indonesian check-in, I was informed that I could not return to Manila without an onward ticket for travel back out of the country. I explained that I lived and worked in Manila and was not planning to leave hence the lack of an onward ticket. They made me wait until all of the other passengers had gone through and then once again other staff members appeared to discuss my case. They phoned Manila immigration who unhelpfully stated that I would need an onward ticket. I was forced to buy the cheapest onward ticket knowing I would never use it.

I arrived back in Manila, passed straight through immigration with NO request for the onward ticket that I had been made to buy. I joined the very long queue for taxis to get home. Reaching my house and collapsing into a chair after my ordeal, I opened my email. To my dismay, I now discovered that after I had already flown, Bravofly had decided that my debit card was acceptable after all and had debited my account. I had therefore paid for the first one-way flight to Bali three times including the original flight that I had missed! A few days later, I lost a larger amount of money in an online identity scam trying to help someone that I thought I knew. I had reached out after being convicted by my Bible reading that day about giving generously.

I guess the moral of this story could be any or all of the following; missionaries shouldn't take holidays, foreigners are an easy target, Filipinos don't want people to enter their country but once they are there they don't want them to leave, immigration issues are a nightmare the world over, Bible verses taken out of context and applied literally to a random situation can be dangerous. More likely, it is that money and material resources need to be held loosely and should not grip our hearts.

CHAPTER THIRTY-TWO

Luxurious Living

Having initially wanted to live in community, I now found that I needed some personal space. It felt a bit like I was living under a microscope as due to being the only foreigner in the area, my every move was discussed by church members. Family members of my housemates had moved in with them and more dogs had begun appearing. We were always on the edge of the contract I had signed which stipulated a maximum of seven adults.

Mums and grandmas were now making a life's work out of keeping our house spotless at all times of the day and night. If I put a dirty bowl or plate down for a few seconds it was immediately scooped up and thoroughly cleaned by one of the many keen ladies who didn't have much else to do. I hadn't minded at first, I had even enjoyed the pampering a bit, although I was concerned about the landlord's reaction to the appearance of the dogs. But, my health was fluctuating which sometimes made it tough to be around others. So, eventually I made the decision to take a short-term contract on a pretty upmarket condo unit with a swimming pool. I thought that moving out might give me some perspective about my life and ministry in Manila.

On moving day, Marshmallow, one of the dogs, was sadly run over in the street right outside the house. Nobody really knew what to do so his little white body just lay there in the street awaiting a decision. Upset by this and about moving out, I was traumatised still further when one of my housemates who hadn't been present for the move phoned to ask me to intervene in an argument that was taking place in my former household about who would have my bed!

The condo unit was peaceful and a novelty at first, but I did feel lonely. I was fifteen floors up with a view of the city. I stood on my balcony staring out over the buildings and watching the activity of all of the people far below. The swimming pool was in the centre of the four tower blocks and most of the balconies over-looked it. Unfortunately, I became the centre of attention again as often alone, I kept up my fifty lengths in the pool every few days.

The worst side effect of my relocation was the possibility of the homeless people seeing me entering or leaving the luxury apartment block. I even resorted to hiding behind a pillar one day when I saw a drop-in attendee digging around on the ground for the remnants of someone else's discarded cigarette right outside the entrance to my tower. The embarrassment and shame I felt in that moment are difficult to describe. I realised that I had probably prided myself on living simply, and now I constantly felt the need to explain to people that my new living situation was just a temporary arrangement.

One positive thing that resulted from my living in the new area were my brief encounters with a very old beggar man nearby. I often passed him and began giving him a bit of loose change whenever I did so. He was too old to be taking drugs or drinking and looked like he should have been resting in a home somewhere rather than wandering the dirty streets for the remainder of his days. My personal policy was always to say something about my faith whenever I did this. I told the man that Jesus loved him and cared about his life. I also gave him details of my church. I was so encouraged when he enthusiastically approached me one day and said that he would always remember what I had told him about Jesus and that he was planning to check out the church.

Living in such luxury did make me feel terribly guilty even though it was just short-term. It reminded me that my attempts to experience poverty by living amongst the people I was working with in Manila, would never be authentic. Most Filipinos would never be able to afford to travel abroad and confined their brief vacations to their own country. I could always leave when things got tough or take a "well deserved" break anywhere in the world.

CHAPTER THIRTY-THREE

Hypothermic in Sagada

In relation to holidays, I was asked to join one of my former housemates and some other girls from the church on one of their short vacations. The small group of us waited for the bus late at night in an outside partial shelter that seemed to be in the middle of nowhere. There was a small TV for entertainment but I would rather they had turned it off as it was prolonged coverage of the annual *Miss World* competition. Scantily clad ladies parading around and being judged on their levels of aesthetic perfection—Miss *World* summed it up perfectly. A Filipino was crowned after the organisers had nearly caused a diplomatic crisis by mistakenly giving the award to the wrong woman.

The Filipino's didn't bat an eye-lid when the bus was several hours late. It wasn't uncommon for people to turn up an hour or more after the start of a prearranged meeting. Tardiness was usually blamed on the traffic rather than disorganisation. It was frustrating, especially when waiting in the street for someone, but changing an entire culture's worth of lateness was probably outside the scope of my missionary brief. I adapted, what other option was there?

We wore numerous layers including thick hoodies on the bus due to the air conditioning blasting continuously from the vents. Once again I was perplexed. I knew we were heading to a colder area, but why did that mean that the bus needed to be so cold. Was there a gradual temperature adaptation issue that I was unaware of?

Arriving in Sagada, we discovered that we needed to join an official tour to even remain in the area. Those who didn't sign up to one of the packages within sufficient time of arrival were hunted down and effectively evicted. That's one way to keep your official tourism figures up.

For our first tour, we walked out into the countryside following the trail of many who had gone before us. Walking up hills and down into valleys, it was bizarre to hear adults hollering random and heavily accented English words which echoed around. We came to an abrupt standstill where a large group of people had congregated. There were tour guides milling around and most groups were in the process of arranging their selfie sticks and snapping multiple photos. Moving to the front of the pack, I looked around for the attraction but could see only a sharp incline and a lot of people standing perilously close to the edge of it. Glancing up, I finally observed that there were a number of coffins and a single wooden chair attached to the cliff face, and hanging directly in front of the area where we were standing. Our guide said that it was considered a great honour to be laid in one of these coffins. I tried to keep my bewilderment to myself as I knew it wasn't culturally appropriate to ask what the purpose was especially when it related to such a sensitive subject as death. I didn't get it, but there were a lot of things about the Philippines that fell into this category and sometimes it was best not to ask.

On another day, we went to see a waterfall. Although I didn't have my swimming gear or a towel, I was tempted when our guide said that a quick dip would probably be okay. I removed my shoes and outer layer and after sitting on the slippery rocks for a while, willed myself to slide into the murky depths. I gasped, it was freezing. I knew I should keep moving around and decided to make the most of it by swimming under the waterfall. The water crashed down on my head, it was refreshing, but quite a few people were now watching and I wasn't warming up. I clambered out and went to sit on a nearby rock to dry off a little.

Watching my friends dangling their legs in the water and chatting a few metres away, I suddenly became aware that my teeth were chattering. I had been feeling fine at first, but I now started shivering violently and couldn't stop. I called out to my friends that I really needed to leave or find a way to get warm. One of them helped me remove some of the wet clothing without making too much of a spectacle. But, I continued to shake and started feeling quite ill. A local man looking worried, commented to our guide that they needed to get me up the hill "immediately."

My companions then realised that my plight might be serious and we all set off back to our pick-up point. I found that I couldn't walk more than a few steps without having to stop for a rest and my breathing had become very heavy and loud. I felt light headed and sick although something had been wrapped around my head to keep the heat in. Finally, reaching the top of the hill and making it back to the car, it took me an age to warm up. Relieved, I later realised that I had probably experienced the on-set of hypothermia. A new experience to add to my growing collection, but not something I planned to repeat. I realised that with an under-active thyroid which made me feel the cold more than most, it had been pretty foolish to go into the water in the first place.

The next day, I opted to remain behind when the others went climbing and trekking again. Unfortunately, the owners of the establishment became worried about the welfare of the "white visitor staying upstairs who had hidden in their room all day." They saw it as their cultural duty to ensure that I had the best and most enjoyable stay I could possibly have whilst in their care. They kept asking whether I was ill and why I didn't like Sagada. When my friends returned, they suggested that I go and explain to the anxious hosts how much I *had* enjoyed my visit and been blessed by their hospitality.

We headed to the bus terminal in order to purchase our tickets home for the following day. By this stage, however, I had had enough of playing tourist in the cold weather, so when I saw a bus labelled Cubao it was too much of a temptation to resist. Despite it being very late in the evening, and it being an eight hour journey back to Cubao, I took short term leave of my senses, said goodbye to my friends and hastened towards the waiting bus. I hadn't anticipated that the bus would be full with standing room only. In the event, the kind conductor gave up his seat at the front of the bus for me for most of the journey and either stood or sat in the aisle himself! The journey was a little like being in a racing car computer simulation. I was at the very front of a gigantic bus, staring out into the night as we sped along with the roads racing past. I was filled with a mixture of fascination and fear. My proximity to the screen magnified everything and the pace was truly frightening but somehow I felt safe. The driver had the voice of experience.

It wasn't until we were a few towns away that I realised I was on the wrong bus and that it wouldn't be going anywhere near Cubao. I began to panic—I was in an unfamiliar place, it was still the middle of the night and I was about to get dropped off somewhere probably by a roadside. Hesitating and feeling slightly foolish, I eventually told the driver and conductor who immediately concocted a clever plan to make sure I got home safely. Having sighted a taxi heading towards us on the other side of the road, they slowed the bus sufficiently to flag it down and allow me to alight. I was swiftly ushered off the rolling bus and before I knew what was happening found myself in the back of the still moving taxi and heading in the opposite direction. Glancing around, I discovered that my belongings had been thrown in after me by the enthusiastic conductor. The bus was already a long way down the road.

On reflection, I realised that I hadn't even had a chance to thank the crew for their actions which were well beyond the call of duty. Their collective efforts were also unusual in a culture where a lot of the people lacked initiative or the confidence to act on it. Whatever the reason for their timely intervention, I was more than grateful especially when I arrived safely home.

CHAPTER THIRTY-FOUR

Decision Time

I mentioned in my introduction that I ended up leaving the Philippines just two years after I had moved to Manila. I have not returned to date and am unsure whether I will be able to. I still believe I am called to full-time mission work, with a particular emphasis on evangelism but at the moment I'm unclear about exactly where God wants me.

My initial call to the Philippines was to work with the "rugby boys" and longer term to possibly provide an institution for them to be accommodated. This work had been halted primarily because of the advice of my pastor due to the fact that the boys had grown older. I couldn't find others with a special heart for the boys to assist me with the work. After the failed attempt to provide housing for Paul and Joel, I also became convinced that lumping them all together in one building away from the streets and people they knew may not be in their best interests longer term.

Ultimately, I was satisfied that all of the boys had heard the Gospel clearly and seen God's love in action through our care for them. They had been introduced to a church in Olongapo with members that had a heart for them. They knew they would be welcome if they decided to attend. It was time to let go.

They still contacted me from time to time on social media and it was by this avenue that I heard the news that Simon, still just fourteen years old, had suffered a heart attack. He had been found by Centre for Youth staff clutching his heart and with no pulse. Despite this he had been released to the custody of his father who had no financial capability at all due to having polio and being unable to work. Simon didn't seem to be taking what had happened to him seriously at all and despite the fact that I made sure he was adequately supplied with medicine he often failed to take it. I felt a sense of dread on hearing the news, awaiting what I thought was the inevitable outcome of Simon's recklessness. But thankfully my fears weren't realised and a few years down the line, Simon lives on. As far as I am aware, all of the boys from my original group are still alive. I often pray that God will protect them if only until their eyes are opened to the truth of the Gospel. God is patient and gracious!

I had subsequently turned my attention to the various outreaches from the church—the drop in, Monday night Bible studies, the Tacloban medical mission, the church plant in Valenzuela and the assistance of a number of individuals who happened to cross my path. But, I was still finding that there was not enough work to keep me busy. I was not a qualified social worker so was unable to become more involved in Christian Compassion Ministries although I spent a fair bit of time editing their English reports. I had a better grasp of the language but not sufficiently to engage in Bible studies in the community. I wondered what God would have me do as the plans that I had had seemed to have unravelled.

Not feeling useful was tricky for me, but it wasn't what caused my decision to take a break from which I didn't return. It was very difficult to form equal friendships with my peers and members in the church. There were a few exceptions, but I found that due to being white and people knowing that I had money, I was treated differently. Some befriended me for these reasons. Others avoided me preferring to stay within their own nationality or feeling too shy to reach out. The Filipino men sometimes competed for interaction with me leaving me feeling confused and unsure of myself. I didn't know who I could trust in a culture where it can be usual practice to gossip rather than speak to someone directly. I'm not going to say any more than this here, but I faced enormous challenges some of which God helped me overcome, and others which tested me to my limits.

My purpose for being in the Philippines had been removed. Some might say the mission in relation to the "rugby boys" had been accomplished. I wanted to stay there and be involved in other work as despite the cultural challenges, I had grown to love the country and people. Thinking about it now, more than anything else, it was my sense of calling that held me there and stopped me leaving earlier. What I had failed to appreciate was that although a person could have a long-term call to mission work, it didn't have to be in a specific place for the duration. Reading older biographies, I realised that missionaries often moved around for seasons when doors closed. This was what appeared to have happened to me.

It was time for Gideon's fleece test. On a whim and with a prayer, I contacted a manager I had worked with on the Logos Hope. Andy was now working at Operation Mobilisation's warehouse in Florence, South Carolina. With little notice, I asked whether I could volunteer there for three months effective immediately. I prayed that if they had accommodation for me that would be my confirmation. After consultation with a few less people than should have been informed judging by a sudden flurry of emails after the event, Andy encouraged me to come.

Although technically, my trip to Florence was only going to be a short break, I guess I knew in my heart that I might not return. I decided to give away all of my belongings, including my entire library which by this point had been completely transferred from England. I was happy to let go of my worldly possessions but knew it would be harder to leave the people.

In order to move some of my larger furniture out of the condominium, I hired a truck with two men. We drove all over town delivering bits and pieces. Stopping at the house of a lady who often cooked large quantities of food for church events, I was horrified to see that her fridge that I had offered to replace was completely black with mould. I wondered that it was still functioning, and that no one had been poisoned, as she indicated that she had been using it for several decades. The dear lady was so excited on receiving the gifts and an unexpected microwave that she followed me and the young hired men out onto the street with plates of spaghetti that had been hastily assembled. We were expected to consume these whilst hanging off the back of the truck containing all my belongings. I tried to insist that I return later knowing that the men were being paid for their time and had already eaten, but she wasn't having any of it. We wolfed down the food before speeding off before she could offer us anything else. Needless to say, when I next saw her at church she was still ecstatic about the items. I was humbled by her gratitude.

On the day of my departure, I experienced a final bureaucratic annoyance. I was attempting to leave my apartment with my suitcases to go to the airport. I was informed I would need to obtain a permit to remove items from the building. The administration office was closed. Exhausted by the past few months and wanting just to get it all over with, I pointed out that I had requested the permit for the weekend prior to my flight and had already removed the bulk of my furniture. I had actually asked if it would be okay to take the last few smaller items during the week and had been told that would be fine. Now it was not fine.

I waited with a few items, an electric fan and a cardboard box as I recall, and a few friends, for around thirty minutes whilst the staff dallied around phoning various supervisors and the carpark guards to try and locate my permit. On managing to hail a taxi I told them that I would be leaving with my suitcases regardless as I had a flight to catch. My friends would wait with the final two items for them to resolve the anomaly. Finally, they found the paper in the nick of time and I was able to prove that yes, I had been telling the truth all along, these were my items and no I wasn't trying to con anyone.

My friend Mabel accompanied me to the airport where there was the usual confusion about wrong terminal numbers and different airlines. On parting, she handed me a letter, I read it after she had gone whilst I was still in the check-in queue and promptly burst into tears. I was going to miss these people.

CHAPTER THIRTY-FIVE

Reverse Culture Shock

My intention was to fly straight from Manila to Florence and then after three months to return to England prior to heading back to the Philippines if God led. However, due to passport expiry issues I had to head to England first. I ended up travelling to Florence a total of three times and spending eight of the following twelve months there. I enjoyed the physical work and the chance to work with literature again. However, the door was closed when I was detained at American immigration on my third visit and told that I must have a work VISA to return. Maybe I just attract immigration officers.

So, I came "home" to a new family house as my parents had moved from West Sussex to Banbury in Oxfordshire during my time abroad. My house in Worthing, West Sussex still had long term tenants. I spent the first week hiding from the cold and laughing at my Filipino friends who thought it was cold in Manila—I checked Google and it was twenty-eight degrees! Bizarrely the quietness in my parent's new dwelling felt almost painful to my ears as I had grown accustomed to the twenty-four-seven noisiness in my apartment in Cubao.

On braving the cold and venturing out, I took a trip to see my sister near Leamington Spa and to meet yet another nephew for the first time. It was great to see them and catch up, but as usual I felt overwhelmed by the whirlwind of activity and wondered for the sixty-fifth thousandth time how on earth my sister coped so well with four kids under the age of five and kept a virtually spotless house. I thought again how different our lives were and also not for the first time was relieved it was she and not me dealing with the resulting chaos.

It felt strange being back in England and I noticed how much things seemed to have advanced even in that short time period; food was more expensive, gadgets more complicated and contactless technology everywhere, making me afraid that I might inadvertently purchase something! In fact, the busyness of life felt immediately stressful compared to the relaxed pace in Manila. Upon visiting Manila as a foreigner, you may not "feel" the difference. There are also large crowds and a lot of activity, but the pace is slower, people are less demanding and the cost of living can be reduced probably by a factor of four! Now, I stood patiently at various service counters anticipating long waits but was unprepared, disconcerted and at times speechless when immediately attended to. My family commented on the "traffic jam" which was approximately five vehicles long, as my mind wandered to the miles of stationary traffic in Manila at all times of the day and night.

I had spent more time in the Philippines over the previous five years than in England. It was one of the reasons I believed I would find it very hard to live in the UK permanently again. It's just not fair to be silently judging others for their standard of living and life choices when they haven't experienced living amongst those suffering the daily strain of poverty and deprivation. To be unconsciously or at times consciously comparing each purchase with its equivalent food or clothing item in the Philippines or even the equivalent cost of life saving medical treatment for the many out there in need.

I heard a phrase on TV; "orientated towards a culture other than one's own" and wondered if that described me, although I think they were talking about buildings. I pondered whether I had always been a misfit for Western living. I concluded that it probably started when I came to faith in 2005, so many of the things that I had been seeking happiness in became worthless at that moment, including most material things. Rather than them creeping back into my life over time, I found less and less satisfaction in them to the point that I detested shopping malls and didn't want to buy anything or spend any money on myself EVER!

My return to England felt a little like walking around in a dream world without a resting place. I was aware of everyday activities and conversations happening around me but I wasn't really sure if I was taking part or just observing. It seemed that so many of the things going on were unimportant. I was told "it's important to keep busy" and that I needed to find things to occupy myself, but I wondered why. I guess I was experiencing reverse culture shock.

I travelled around the country visiting family members and friends and the time spent catching up felt worthwhile. I was encouraged by the consistency of Christian friends and also by some relatively new believers persevering in the Christian battle, one who commented dejectedly "Nat, the Christian life is hard!" A Christian who is finding life easy is usually doing something wrong. I was also reminded of things I had said to people in the past which I was now forgetting to apply to my own life struggles and difficulties. How easy it is to forget and to repeat past mistakes only to be forced to learn the same lessons again and again. God is so very patient with me.

Reflecting, I realised that the frenetic busyness and never-ending lists of tasks that "must" be done could act as a permanent distraction for some people. It could stop them thinking about and spending time on or with the important things in life; people, relationships, faith. There were no doubt things that needed to be done and sitting around pondering life was not a luxury granted to everyone. It would probably also lead to poor mental and physical health if carried out for extended periods. I was reminded again of a conclusion I had previously come to about materialism:

"The more things we accumulate, the more cluttered our lives become, and the more stressed we feel as we are compelled to think about them. Life is about people not about things."

The Bible puts it like this;

"Do not love the world or the things in the world. If anyone loves the world, the love of the Father is not in him. For all that is in the world—the desires of the flesh and the desires of the eyes and pride of life—is not from the Father but is from the world. And the world is passing away along with its desires, but whoever does the will of God abides forever." 1 John 2 vs 15-17 (ESV)

There is only one question that remains to be answered; is it really more fun in the Philippines? I'm sure you have formed your own conclusions having read about some of my experiences. It is undoubtedly *different* and *more unusual* for a Westerner living in the Philippines, but more fun? The answer probably lies in your personal definition of "fun", therefore it is entirely subjective. There are positive aspects of Filipino culture and negative ones, the same as there would be in any culture or people group.

The wild and unpredictable weather may be at least partly responsible for the "live for the moment" mindset which is so alien to us Westerners with our retirement funds and forward planning. According to Wikipedia, *"approximately twenty tropical cyclones enter the Philippine Area of Responsibility yearly of which ten will be typhoons with five being destructive. The Philippines is "the most exposed country in the world to tropical storms"* It is entirely possible that Filipinos are living for the moment because they are unconsciously thinking that they might only have that moment left!

We are all a product of the culture we live in. The only true commonality amongst people, tribes and nations all over the world is our need of a Saviour from sin. We have all sinned and fallen short of the glory of God. We stand in need of His rescue. Thankfully God has already provided Jesus, His perfect sacrifice for our sin. Whether Filipino, English, Chinese, Australian or American, we can be restored to Him and have new life in heaven forever.

About the Author

Natalie was raised in a Christian home in West Sussex, England to parents Keith and Kim Vellacott. She had two younger siblings, James and Lauren. She professed faith in Christianity at a young age but fell away from God at seventeen, having just been baptised. Natalie subsequently spent many years living a worldly lifestyle before being definitely converted at the age of twenty-three.

Career wise, Natalie joined Sussex Police as an officer when she was just nineteen. Within the police, she worked in many departments including Uniform response and patrol, CID (as a detective,) Child Protection and Internal Investigations. After her conversion to Christianity in 2005, Natalie continued to work for Sussex Police and was promoted to Sergeant in 2009. Natalie's autobiography *Planet Police* was published in late 2015 by Onwards and Upwards.

Natalie found it increasingly difficult to be a Christian in a secular work environment and her focus was gradually changed to mission work. She took part in street evangelism in her spare time and spent many hours sharing her faith with colleagues at work. In 2011, Natalie felt that God was calling her to apply for a two-year commitment on the Logos Hope Christian Missionary Ship. She applied for a two-year career break from Sussex Police, which was granted, and was subsequently accepted for the Mission, after initially being told she might have to go to Afghanistan instead!

Natalie fulfilled her two-year commitment on the Logos Hope and wrote about it in *The Logos Life*. As a result of her experiences whilst on-board, she subsequently moved to live and work in the Philippines as an independent Missionary in December 2013. Natalie served for several years in Metro Manila, working with the street homeless people and teenagers who abuse solvents. *They're Rugby*

Boys, Don't You Know? published in 2014, was Natalie's debut novel about her journey with some Filipino street boys.

Natalie returned to England in early 2016 and has been working as a volunteer for Need Him/Chat Now UK, a Christian online chat facility sharing Jesus with people all around the world. She has also spent several months volunteering at an Operation Mobilisation warehouse that supplies books to the Logos Hope, based in Florence, USA. In addition to reading avidly and writing honest, Christian perspective book reviews, Natalie blogs about contemporary Christian issues at www.christianmissionaryuk.blogspot.co.uk.

Natalie often uses her personal story as a living testimony of the hope that can be found only in Jesus, inspiring others to seek Him as their source of hope. She seeks to help people find assurance in God's promise of eternal life through the verse in Romans 10 vs 9 *"If you confess with your mouth Jesus is Lord and believe in your heart God raised Him from the dead, you WILL be saved."*

Natalie's Personal Story

I became a Christian at a young age primarily due to having been raised in a Christian home and being surrounded by Christianity. As a teenager there were times when I was really serious about my faith. But there were also times when I became distracted from God and I wasn't really building a personal relationship with Him. During a more serious faith phase at the age of seventeen I was baptised by full immersion, but just six weeks later fell away from God in a dramatic fashion.

I subsequently spent six years immersed in the "party lifestyle", succumbing to many activities and bad habits that sought to replace God, including an abundance of alcohol, cigarettes, gambling, and the regular watching of violent/horror movies. I moved from one non-Christian relationship to another in an attempt to find happiness which eluded me. I became more and more miserable attempting to ignore God, but knowing deep down that He was really there and that I was under His judgement because of my lifestyle choices.

I began a course in Law and Criminology at Sheffield University in 2000, but dropped out after just six weeks to join Sussex Police, thereby fulfilling a childhood dream. In 2002, my younger brother James (who was a Christian) was tragically killed in a car accident at the age of just eighteen. My parents clung to their Christian faith at this time, but I became angry with God for allowing this to happen and resented others for judging my lifestyle.

In April 2005, after many other problems and a long struggle, I faced up to the fact that I was miserable and that my life was a total mess. I had recently witnessed my younger sister Lauren going through a mini-version of the same struggles and had seen the resulting contentment when God graciously called her back to Himself and Lauren repented and trusted in Him. I knew that I was carrying the heavy weight of my many sins around on my shoulders every day. I sometimes woke up at night in a terrified state, believing I was going to hell because of the things I had done. I knew that God was waiting for me to repent of my sin and turn back to Him and that He had been patiently waiting for a long time. I lived in constant fear that time would run out and that I may have tested God's grace one too many times. Eventually, God brought me to the end of my resources. All I could do was cry out for His help. I said sorry to God for my many sins. I believed His promise that, 'All who call on the name of the Lord will be saved'. God, by His grace, planted true faith in my heart and I determined to live a new life before Him.

I abandoned my sinful vices immediately and began regularly attending my former church: Worthing Tabernacle. Two Bible verses became very important to me as a result of my experiences. The first is found in John 6 vs 67-68 *"You do not want to leave too, do you?" Jesus asked the Twelve. Simon Peter answered him, "Lord, to whom shall we go? You have the words of eternal life."* (NIV) These verses remind me that seeking anyone other than Jesus is a total waste of time because He is the only one with the words of eternal life that can offer hope for the future. The second verse is from Mark 8 vs 36 *"For what shall it profit a man, if he shall gain the whole world, and lose his own soul?"* (KJV) This sums up my life experience as I tried seeking happiness in the world but foolishly risked losing my soul in the process.

When I tell people my story I am often asked "How do you know it was God who brought you back to your faith and not just a decision you made and carried out through your own will and determination?" This is a good question. The truth is that I didn't have the strength or desire to give up my vices, I tried many times to turn my life around and always failed. Although I saw the emptiness and meaninglessness of life without God and the utter futility of daily life lived without purpose, I was powerless to make the big changes I knew were necessary. I was so immersed in my sinful lifestyle that a new start seemed like an impossibility. Before God could help me I had to accept that I needed His help, that I was totally dependent and reliant on Him to restore me and that I couldn't change anything myself. True salvation occurs only when God changes a person's heart allowing them to believe in Him. The Bible says in Matthew 19 vs 26 *"With man this is impossible, but with God all things are possible."*

God already had His hand on my life, due to my Christian upbringing, former beliefs and the fact that many people were praying for me regularly. God protected me from serious harm throughout this period and from serious long term consequences. Looking back, I am so grateful to God for the mercy, grace and patience that He demonstrated towards me during my rebellion. The Bible says in Ephesians 2 vs 8-9 *"By grace you have been saved, through faith and that not of yourselves; it is the gift of God; not of works, lest any man should boast."* This is my personal experience and all of the glory for the change in my life goes to God as I wasn't capable of turning my own life around.

The Wordless Book

I wouldn't be a true evangelist without explaining what it means to become a Christian and how you too can be free of your sin and reconciled to God to spend eternity in heaven with Him one day.

During my last few years of missionary service I was taught a tool to explain the Gospel. It has been effectively used by millions of people around the world. It is called the *Wordless Book* and consists simply of five coloured sheets of paper or material each representing part of the message of salvation found in the Bible.

Yellow: This represents heaven. Do you want everlasting life in Heaven?

The Bible tells us that the streets in heaven are paved with gold. It also tells us that God is light and that in Him there is no darkness and that Jesus (God's only Son) is the light of the world. Heaven is God's dwelling place and the Bible also tells us that no man has ever imagined the wonderful things that God has prepared in heaven for those that love Him.

Heaven is forever.

Black: This represents sin. What is wrong with the world? More importantly, what is wrong with me?

Being honest, we need to face the bad news in order to see the value of the good news. The Bible says that all people have sinned and fall short of the glory of God and that the wages of sin is death.

God is holy and cannot have anything to do with sin. God is righteous and just and therefore cannot just overlook our sin and forgive us because this would make Him unjust. Our sin separates us from God permanently. All sinners are destined to spend an eternity in hell without God. Hell is a truly terrible place where people will long to die because of their torment but will be unable to do so.

Hell is forever.

This is the bad news.

Red: This represents the blood of Jesus. Why did Jesus need to die?

God loved us so much that He provided a way of for us to be reconciled to Him and to escape the torments of hell. He sent Jesus His only son to live a perfect life here on earth. It was necessary for a penalty to be paid for our sin. Jesus' purpose in coming was to allow Himself to be sacrificed and punished on a cross in the place of all who believe that He died for them, and who put their trust in Him.

He died instead of them so that they could be free from the guilty sentence hanging over them because of their sin. He died on that cross and then rose from the grave just three days later proving that He had defeated sin and death once and for all. Jesus' death acted as a bridge between guilty sinners and God allowing all who trust in Him to be forgiven for their sins and to live in heaven forever with God.

White: This represents being washed clean from sin. How can be we sure of God's acceptance?

Think of your life as a white sheet. Every time you sin, even in a small way, a black stain is left on the sheet. When a person becomes a Christian and turns away from their sin, God promises them a new start. He says that he will remember their sins no more.

When God looks at the life of a Christian he sees only Jesus and His righteousness instead of the sin.

Green: This represents growth. How should this change my life?

All true Christians will grow spiritually over time. In order to grow, Christians should regularly read the word of God (the Bible,) pray, attend a church, spend time with other Christians and tell other people about Jesus and His sacrifice for them.

These things do not save people. There are no "divine scales" weighing good and bad deeds as a determining factor for entry to heaven or hell. No human can ever do enough good things to get to heaven as the standard required is perfection, which is why Jesus had to die.

The things described here are the grateful response of a Christian who has been rescued from a life of sin and death and reconciled to God for a life of hope and an eternal future in heaven.

Please contact me at natalie.vellacott@gmail.com if you would like further information.

Asian Adventures, Cultural Catastrophes, Help and Hope
On-board the World's Largest Floating Book-Fair!

The LOGOS Life

Natalie Vellacott

Printed in Great Britain
by Amazon